Sacred
TENACITY

56 DAYS
········· *of* ·········
Practicing Perseverance
and Embracing God's
Faithfulness

HEATHER DILLARD

Sacred Tenacity: 56 Days of Practicing Perseverance and Embracing God's Faithfulness by Heather Dillard

Scripture quotations marked CEV are taken from the CONTEMPORARY ENGLISH VERSION (CEV): Scripture taken from the CONTEMPORARY ENGLISH VERSION copyright© 1995 by the American Bible Society. Used by permission.

Scripture quotations marked ESV are from The ESV® Bible (The Holy Bible, English Standard Version®), copyright © 2001 by Crossway, a publishing ministry of Good News Publishers. Used by permission. All rights reserved.

Scripture quotations marked NIV are taken from the Holy Bible, NEW INTERNATIONAL VERSION®, NIV® Copyright © 1973, 1978, 1984, 2011 by Biblica, Inc.® Used by permission. All rights reserved worldwide.

Scripture quotations marked NLT are taken from the HOLY BIBLE, NEW LIVING TRANSLATION (NLT): Scriptures taken from the HOLY BIBLE, NEW LIVING TRANSLATION, Copyright© 1996, 2004, 2007 by Tyndale House Foundation. Used by permission of Tyndale House Publishers, Inc., Carol Stream, Illinois 60188. All rights reserved. Used by permission.

Edited by Sam O'Neal
Front cover and interior layout design by Krista Joy Johnson

ISBN-13: 978-0-9992289-2-0 (paperback)
ISBN-13: 978-0-9992289-3-7 (ePub e-book)
ISBN-13: 978-0-9992289-4-4 (.mobi e-book)

Published by Heather Dillard

To the one who needs strength to fight another day.
...May your heart be encouraged.

TABLE OF Contents

Introduction

The hospital room would have been white and cold, if it wasn't for the pink azaleas and other green plants crowding the windowsill. A giant whiteboard stared down at me, notating that shifts had changed and a new set of nurses were about to come in for the day. A complementary rose-colored plastic bucket sat to my right on the single cabinet that served as a nightstand. The bucket was filled with white gauze, medical tape, and bottles of sterile water solution for wound care. The bed sheets and pillow smelled like bleach.

Soon a young man with medium brown hair came into the room. He introduced himself as my physical therapist for the day. Instead of simply doing exercises from the bed, today he was going to help me get up and move around.

After a life-saving surgery to remove my colon, followed by eight days in ICU (six of those days in a medically-induced coma), this would be the first time I'd been out of my bed in almost three weeks. I had just finished my junior year of college. Due to medical complications, my body had been pumped full of fluid, and my arms and legs had swollen tremendously. After a couple weeks, my arms had regained their normal appearance, but my legs still felt like weighted sausages.

"Alright, let's get started," the physical therapist spoke to me. He helped me heave my swollen legs to the side of the hospital bed. "Let's go from the bed to the chair first."

I leaned on his shoulder while I tried to put weight on my legs, then collapsed back onto the bed. "I feel like a baby elephant!" I wailed.

Have your legs ever fallen asleep, and they feel like lead balloons when you try to put weight on them? This felt similar, only ten times worse. *I can't do this*, I thought. *It's too hard.* I could feel tears beginning to sting my eyes. The physical therapist graciously gave me a minute to pull myself together. I took a deep breath. We tried again. I was able to pivot into the waiting chair nearby.

Within a few days, the real work began. First, I stood at the sink and brushed my teeth. Then I started taking short walks down the hall with a walker, a cloth belt wrapped around my waist that the physical therapist held for my safety. One day I made it all the way down the hall. The day we decided to walk all the way around the nurses' station, I remember telling the physical therapist next to me, "Start talking with me so I can get distracted and not think about how hard this is."

Sometimes we just have to take one step at a time. I don't know what season you find yourself in right now. Maybe you've suffered a horrible loss and find it hard to get out of bed in the morning. Maybe you're a mom with young kids, you're drowning in laundry and toys, and your patience is wearing thin. Maybe you've just been given a gut-wrenching diagnosis. You need a glimmer of encouragement, a speck of hope in the chaos.

Well, you've picked up the right book. I have been praying for those who will receive this book, and I believe you have this in your hands for a reason. Specifically, this book will help you engage God's biblical call to persevere.

What is perseverance? It isn't about putting your head down, gritting your teeth, putting your shoulder to the wheel, and ignoring the pain. It's not about denial. True perseverance is honest about the pain. It's real and authentic. A persevering person acknowledges the pain and struggle, but in the midst of it chooses to get up and fight another day.

You can't continue to persevere in your own strength. But you do have a choice every day. And when we choose each day to listen to what God is saying and follow in His footsteps, then we are filled with confidence and peace and contentment knowing that our Father knows the way and will guide us on the right paths.

In Lamentations 3, we see a bold, honest picture of what it looks like to persevere:

> *"I tell myself, 'I am finished! I can't count on the Lord to do anything for me.' Just thinking of my troubles and my lonely wandering makes me miserable. That's all I ever think about, and I am depressed. Then I remember something that fills me with hope. The Lord's kindness never fails! If he had not been merciful, we would have been destroyed. The Lord can always be trusted to show mercy each morning. Deep in my heart I say, 'The Lord is all I need; I can depend on him!'"* (Lamentations 3:18–24, CEV)

There it is. This man is hopeless and miserable and depressed. *But then I remember something that fills me with hope.* God is always faithful. He is constant. He can be trusted. The Lord's kindness never fails.

Perhaps, dear friend, you don't believe God is always faithful or good. Perhaps there are several areas where you need God's mercy to come through for you today. Perhaps you feel miserable, but there is a part in you that wants to remember hope. For the next fifty-six days (that's eight weeks, in case you're wondering), we will be exploring what it means to be honest with our pain, choose to remember hope, and experience the faithful mercy of the Lord.

As you bravely choose to start this journey, may you be encouraged and strengthened to get up and learn to walk again, one day at a time.

Sincerely,

Heather Dillard

> "We don't walk spiritually by electric light, but by a hand-held lantern. And a lantern shows only the next step."
>
> —AMY CARMICHAEL, MISSIONARY TO INDIA

PERSEVERING
in the Little Things

• •

"Never give in. Never, never, never, never–in
nothing, great or small, large or petty–never
give in except to convictions of honor
and good sense."

WINSTON CHURCHILL

DAY 1

What is Perseverance?

"Now may the God of peace Himself sanctify you completely, and may your whole spirit and soul and body be kept blameless at the coming of our Lord Jesus Christ. He who calls you is faithful; He will surely do it."

1 THESSALONIANS 5:23-24

*T*his is not how I thought things would turn out.

    I lay on my back on the bed as a single tear ran down my face and into my ear. *I feel like I'm back to square one. I don't think I can keep doing this.*

Months before, I'd had major surgery on my abdomen, and every day following seemed to be an exercise in tenacity. Each week were doctor's appointments, wound care, and bodily fluid accidents that made me feel like an old person. To say this season was discouraging is an understatement. But I was slowly learning to take one day at a time. One step at a time. One update at a time. Sometimes it felt like two steps forward and one step back. But slowly, each day did get better, and my body got stronger and healthier.

Today, as a Licensed Professional Counselor, I get the privilege of hearing so many people's stories. I realize that not everyone's story turns out for the better; sometimes the story of life can go horrifically wrong for no discernable reason. But I believe continuing to choose perseverance is a major key in whether or not our hearts survive life's thrashings.

Merriam-Webster defines *perseverance* as "continued effort to do or achieve something despite difficulties, failure, or opposition." Sometimes it's really hard to keep going. Sometimes we are persevering through things in life far longer than we ever thought we would.

I don't know what your story is, my friend. Our stories are different. But as I share parts of my own story throughout this book, my prayer is that you may find hope for your story as well. That this common thread will weave itself in between our stories: we can choose perseverance because through everything, God is always faithful. We may not understand everything this life throws at us, but we can know that God never changes and He is always with us.

Now is not the time to throw in the towel. Now is the time to persevere. Will you choose to take the next step with me today?

PRACTICE PERSEVERANCE: Where is one area you need to choose perseverance in your life right now? What steps can you take over the next eight weeks in order to actively choose perseverance and invite God to show His faithfulness in your life?

DAY 2

Your Work Matters

"So, my dear brothers and sisters, be strong and immovable.
Always work enthusiastically for the Lord, for you know
that nothing you do for the Lord is ever useless."

2 CORINTHIANS 15:58 (NLT)

J don't know how many times I've rolled over when my alarm has gone off in the morning and thought, *I don't know if I can do this another day.* No, I am not being suicidal. But I do have days when I am discouraged and I don't feel like starting another day of routines and work and stuff. Sometimes I wonder, *Is what I'm doing really making a difference?*

It's so easy to think that no one ever sees the work you do. No one cares. Whether it's the millions of diapers you change every day, the juggling of chore charts, or the fact that you balance your numbers at the end of the day—it doesn't really matter in the grand scheme of things. Right?

That's a lie.

Each action you take is planting a seed. And that seed is sprouting in the dark soil of somebody's life and soul. They may not know it, and you may not see the results right now, but that seed of faithfulness is growing deeper and stronger.

What you do *does* matter. And it matters *a lot*. Even when nobody sees you or thanks you, what you are doing makes a difference in people's lives. Maybe it's what you get paid to do: accountant, grocery sacker, nurse, bank teller, teacher. *Your work matters.* And maybe what you do every day is not a paying job: stay-at-home mom, caretaker for an elderly parent, student. *Your work matters.*

Each day you show up to work on time is a seed planted. Each word of kindness spoken to encourage someone is a seed planted. Each time you sacrifice yourself for the good of someone else is a seed planted. And those seeds will continue to grow and bear fruit—the fruit of confidence and love and purpose.

You are exactly who you need to be for the place you are at right now. The gifts and talents and dreams and desires God has placed in your heart are there for a reason. You are right where you are supposed to be. As you look around, life probably does not look like you thought it would. But that's okay. It doesn't mean you're in the wrong spot. It means you need to continue to persevere in the place God has you in at this very moment.

He knows the plans He has for you. He has not forgotten you. And nothing you do for the Lord is ever useless.

PRACTICE PERSEVERANCE: What seeds are you planting right now? In what ways are you seeing the fruit of your work growing?

DAY 3

When You Want to Hide

"Dear brothers and sisters, when troubles of any kind come
your way, consider it an opportunity for great joy. For you
know that when your faith is tested, your endurance has a
chance to grow. So let it grow, for when your endurance is fully
developed, you will be perfect and complete, needing nothing."

JAMES 1:2–4 (NLT)

*H*ave you ever heard the phrase "hiding in plain sight"? Like a chameleon, some animals and insects have built-in camouflage that allows them to be out in the open, yet we might walk right past them if we're not looking for them.

But animals and insects aren't the only ones who do this. People hide in plain sight, too. Putting on sunglasses and taking off for a long drive down the road. Staying busy so the pain doesn't surface. Pasting on a smile to pretend everything's okay. Netflix binging, mindless Facebook scrolling, drinking too much.

What are some of the ways you "hide in plain sight"? How do you respond when all you want to do is run away and not face the truth? We all do it at times. I am an introvert, so I tend to withdraw into myself, write in my journal, not talk to people, and keep myself busy. If you're more of an extrovert, you may react differently. Maybe you surround yourself with more people so you don't feel alone, but you can stay talking about "surface" issues and not have to really talk about what's going on deeper inside yourself. Maybe you seek approval through a relationship you know isn't the best for you. Maybe it's a combination of these things.

I've noticed that when I get in these spots, I have to intentionally stop myself and admit what I'm doing. *Okay, I'm really trying to hide from what's going on. I've been scrolling mindlessly through Instagram for thirty minutes. I haven't seen any people outside of work for almost a week. I haven't had a real conversation with a friend since last year's summer vacation.*

Then, I have to decide to face what I'm feeling. Many times I'm in a situation where I feel like a failure, or feel like I have to prove something to someone. Many times I've believed the lie that if I just work harder, then I can fix everything. When I realize this is just digging me into a deeper hole, I have to choose to do one other thing: I invite God into this situation.

Usually I pray something like this:

> *God, I'm believing this lie about myself that I'm not good enough and I'm just going to keep failing at everything. It makes me want to run away and hide. I really don't feel like dealing with this pain. But I can also see that it's not getting me anywhere good. I keep numbing the pain with [fill in the blank—eating or Netflix binging or staying busy or whatever]. Would You please quiet my heart and remind me the truth of what You say about me?*

Then I listen. Sometimes God will immediately speak to my heart, or a Bible verse will come to mind that addresses the issue. (That's the Holy Spirit, by the way. Jesus said in John 14:26 the Holy Spirit will remind us of what God has told us.) Sometimes He helps me "wrap words" around what I'm feeling so that I'm able to process it and get to the truth better. (This might include some sessions with a counselor.) And sometimes He doesn't answer right away, but I will feel His peace wash over me. And maybe He will give me words for it at a later time.

Surrendering our fears and choosing to believe God's truth is hard. It's a constant battle; every day we have a choice of what to listen to. But today, you can choose to believe the truth of what God says, and to accept His peace instead of fear. When your faith is tested, perseverance is coming. *Let it grow in you.*

PRACTICE PERSEVERANCE: How are you trying to hide from the truth? Ask God to show you His truth today, and write down (either on this page or your phone's Notes app) what you sense Him speaking to you.

DAY 4

It's Not Bad, It's Just Different

> "That is why I tell you not to worry about everyday life—
> whether you have enough food and drink, or enough clothes
> to wear. Isn't life more than food, and your body more than
> clothing? Look at the birds. They don't plant or harvest or
> store food in barns, for your heavenly Father feeds them.
> And aren't you far more valuable to Him than they are?"
>
> MATTHEW 6:25-26 (NLT)

*B*efore a high school mission trip I took to Germany, we had a three-day period in the US that was called "base camp." During the trip, we would be interacting with many people of different cultures, so the staff used these three days beforehand to help prepare us for what we might encounter.

One of our cultural lessons during base camp came at meal time. Along with our meal was a glass of some brown, cloudy liquid, with round black balls in the bottom of the cup. The servers were not allowed to answer our questions about the meal. I eyed the glass in front of me. It was cold, with condensation already forming on the outside. A few of my brave team members cautiously sipped the drink or tried to fish the strange black balls out of the bottom. They remarked it tasted like chai tea, and the balls were gummy and licorice-flavored. I did not know what this was, and I wasn't about to taste what could be very nasty black things in the bottom of my glass. Later on, I found out this is called "boba," "pearl," or "bubble" tea, and is actually very common in some parts of the world. It originates from Taiwan and is tea and milk steeped together, with gummy tapioca balls as the "pearls" at the bottom.

After this experiment, one of the leaders challenged us: "You will encounter people of different cultures on this trip. There may be many things that you are not familiar with. But instead of saying, 'That's weird,' tell yourself, 'It's not weird or bad; it's just different.'"

I used to think that I would spend my years after college full-time in another country. I have always been fascinated by other cultures and languages. Due to several circumstances, that is not what I am doing today. I am self-employed in a small town, and I'm still trying to practice my Spanish (and maybe even learn French!). I could have never known that day at base camp, sitting in front of my bubble tea, how differently my life would be from what I pictured.

But I've seen God work out His plans in other ways. I am able to support (with my money and prayers) other people who do have the opportunity to share the gospel in other countries. I am learning that I am called just as powerfully to share Jesus where I am. Right here, today.

My life has turned out nothing like I thought it would. But I think that's how God works sometimes. He puts something on our hearts, and there is almost always a time period between that promise and the completion of it. Some people call it "the gap."

We live in an instant, "microwave" culture, and we want things to happen immediately. But God's timing isn't like that. He will often take years—even lifetimes—before the completion of His promise. Even so, remember: it's not bad; it's just different. The way things have turned out are not bad or wrong. They are just different than we expected.

God knows where you are and what you've been through. And it's going to be okay. Not because everything is perfect, but because you are valuable to Him. He sees the big picture of where all this is headed, and His plans for you are always good.

PRACTICE PERSEVERANCE: What is one area in your life that turned out differently than you planned? Are you able to say about God's plans: "It's not bad, it's just different"?

DAY 5

Enough for Today

"The Lord is my shepherd; I have all that I need. He lets me rest in green meadows; He leads me beside peaceful streams. He renews my strength. He guides me along right paths, bringing honor to His name."

PSALM 23:1-3 (NLT)

Author and theologian Ray Vander Laan has created a series of videos called "That the World May Know." These videos explore specific sites throughout Israel and the surrounding regions, linking the cultural truths of biblical times to present day applications. Some translations of Psalm 23:2 say, "He makes me lie down in green pastures." In one of Vander Laan's lessons on location in the Israeli desert, he explains about where the Israeli shepherds lived. There's not much water there. Extreme temperatures rule the day, and almost-freezing temperatures come at night. There's nothing there that we as Westerners would equate with "green pastures." There is sandy barrenness as far as the eye can see.

But there is a bit of moisture that comes from drops of dew at night, and the Mediterranean Sea blows in moist air toward evening. This creates just enough liquid to soak at the base of the rocks scattered throughout the desert. At the base of these rocks, single tufts of grass will spring up. Then the shepherds will take their flocks along the dusty hills to graze. As the sheep move forward, they encounter the tufts of grass—a little bite here, step forward, a little bite there. The shepherds call this "green pastures."

Vander Laan notes, "In the desert, you learn the shepherd gives you just what you need for right now."[1]

That's provision. How many times do we expect God to give us all we need for the next year or five years? We grow impatient, wanting to know more than just one step ahead. But what if God really is being the Good Shepherd by giving us only what we need for today? It may not look like much, but what is right in front of us is enough. A little here, step forward, a little there. Then we will have to trust the Shepherd to lead us to the next pasture tomorrow.

Choosing to accept God's "enough" for each day is an act of perseverance. What you see in front of you today might look like barren wasteland. But looks can be deceiving. Maybe God wants to take you along green pastures—it just may not look like the rolling green hills that you've pictured.

PRACTICE PERSEVERANCE: What provisions (single "tufts of grass") has God given you for today? Use Psalm 23 as your declarative prayer today, and ask God to help you trust Him as your Shepherd.

[1] *Faith Lessons: Walking with God in the Desert*. DVD. Zondervan, 2011.

PERSEVERING
in Your True Identity

. . . .

"It is not the critic who counts. Not the man
who points out how the strong man stumbles,
or where the doer of deeds could have done
them better. The credit belongs to the man
who is actually in the arena, whose face is
marred by dust and sweat and blood."

THEODORE ROOSEVELT

DAY 6

Get Tenacious

"[David said] 'The Lord who rescued me from the
claws of the lion and the bear will rescue me from
this Philistine!' Saul finally consented. 'All right, go
ahead,' he said. 'And may the Lord be with you!'"

1 SAMUEL 17:37 (NLT)

M
ost likely you are familiar with the story of David and Goliath. If not, let me give you a quick summary. The Israelite army was fighting one of their dreaded enemies, the Philistines, who lived across the valley. One of the Philistine warriors, Goliath, was nine feet tall, with armor and weapons to match. Knowing he had the upper hand in terms of war experience, Goliath came up with an idea. He shouted over at the Israelites (sound carries far in a canyon), "Why don't you send your best man to fight me, one on one? Then whoever wins will force the other side to be their slaves." Of course, no one on the Israelite side volunteered; in fact, they all ran and hid.

Then along came someone unexpected: the youngest brother of three of Israel's strapping warriors. The little brother's name was David. "Hey guys, what's up?" he said (my paraphrase of course). "Dad wanted me to bring you this food. He wants to make sure you are all doing okay." Just then, the warrior Goliath came out again—as he had done every day before—and bellowed his challenge. "I bet Israel and their God could never defeat me!"

"David, what are you doing here?" his brothers hissed. "Go home! This is no place for a little boy! Go back to your little flock of sheep."

But David had heard too much. "Isn't someone going to do something?" he asked. "That man is saying that God and His people are powerless!" Word of David's questioning spread like wildfire throughout the camp, and soon reached the king. King Saul immediately summoned David, but he was put off by how small and young David was. "You're just a boy," he said. "This giant has been practicing war since he was your age."

But David was undeterred. He knew all of his near-death experiences caring for sheep in the middle of the desert has taught him one thing: God is the same out in the desert as He would be on this battleground. David knew who God was, and that meant he knew who he was. That made him tenacious. He did not back down or give any excuses.

I love this definition of the word *tenacious*: "not readily relinquishing a position, principle, or course of action; determined; persisting in existence; not easily dispelled."

Being called "tenacious" may sometimes be seen as a bad thing or an insult. But I think when it comes to perseverance, we do have to be tenacious. We have to be tenacious in who God says He is and who He says we are.

We must fight for the truth of who God says we are, because there are so many voices around us that will argue otherwise. *You're too young. You're too old. You're not smart enough. You don't have enough experience. You're not good enough.* When these lies come, we have to choose right then to get tenacious and fight back with the truth:

- No, God says that I have been given everything I need for living a godly life (2 Peter 1:3).
- I choose to set an example in what I say and the way I live (1 Timothy 2:14).
- God is with me, and He delights in me. He will calm my fears and sing His songs over me (Zephaniah 3:17).

PRACTICE PERSEVERANCE: What lies have you believed about yourself? Write them down. Then use a Bible-search tool (such as the BibleGateway or YouVersion app) to find and write down the truth of what God says about you to counter those lies. Tear off the side of your list with the lies and either tear it up into little pieces or burn it (safely, of course). Pray and ask God to help you to be tenacious and believe what He says about you today.

DAY 7

Covenant of Peace

"'For the mountains may depart and the hills be
removed, but My steadfast love shall not depart from
you, and My covenant of peace shall not be removed,'
says the Lord, who has compassion on you."

ISAIAH 54:10 (ESV)

When I was thirteen, I thought what I loved to do could not possibly line up with what God wanted me to do with my life. I quit ballet lessons after eight years of training because I knew God had called me to be a missionary—and you can't possibly tell people about Jesus while you're a professional ballerina, right? Ok, so maybe I would have never made it to professional ballerina status, but I also think I may have gotten a few things wrong. Life is not as black-and-white as we think it is when we are thirteen years old.

Here's what I would tell my younger self all these years later (and maybe you can learn these lessons quicker than I did):

1) God created you to love the things you love for a reason. He knows exactly how He made you. He knows what makes your heart come alive and what takes your breath away. He made you just as you are *on purpose*. Don't discount the joys He has placed inside you. Yes, we all have days where we have to do things we don't want to do. But don't let those things drown out the passion God has gifted you with.

2) Life won't turn out the way you planned. I can almost guarantee this. Life won't look like you pictured it. But that's okay. It's not bad; it's just different. Embrace it. Be flexible. This is still a hard lesson for me to learn, but the quicker I do learn it, the more peace I have. Things will change, but that's okay. Enjoy living from your heart and learn to roll with the punches along the way. You will have a lot less fear and anxiety when you are at peace with this.

3) You can trust God's heart for you. Just as He made you "you" for a reason, He also has good plans for you (Jeremiah 29:11). That's not just a verse to hang on your refrigerator. It's really true. God created you as a masterpiece, and He has good things for you to do. He also has good things to give you. He's not going to harm you; He's going to bring good to your life.

Just as today's verse from Isaiah says, God's covenant of peace is never going to leave us. But we have to let go of control in order to step into that peace. Choosing to surrender daily and believe what God has promised is part of what it means to persevere. God has compassion on you. He knows what's best for you. And no matter how much things around you change, His love for you will never change and never go away.

So let go of control today. God's got this.

PRACTICE PERSEVERANCE: Is there a part of your life that looks different than you thought it would? Choose to let go of control today and ask that God would settle your heart in His peace. Let His steadfast love and perfect peace wash over you.

DAY 8

What Will You Put On?

"Since God chose you to be the holy people He loves, you
must clothe yourselves with tenderhearted mercy, kindness,
humility, gentleness, and patience. Make allowance for
each other's faults, and forgive anyone who offends you.
Remember, the Lord forgave you, so you must forgive others."

COLOSSIANS 3:12-13 (NLT)

*H*ave you ever looked into your closet and said, "I don't have anything to wear!"? While this tends to be more of a problem with women, my dad has come up with a solution for himself. He has a very basic closet strategy: keep only a few of each type of clothing in the closet. When he wears one shirt, he puts it to the back of his clothes rack and then wears the next available shirt the following day. He says it makes getting dressed a lot simpler.

Believe it or not, the Bible has something to say about what we put on every day. Today's verse isn't talking about your clothes, though. Here in Colossians 3:12–13, the apostle Paul is talking about our attitudes and hearts. What are we choosing to pick up and put on today?

There are seven basic items in this wardrobe:

1. Identity (verse 12). There is a reason this is listed first. Don't miss it. The apostle Paul states: You are chosen and holy and dearly loved. We have to know who we are before we can continue on with the rest of Paul's instructions. That's why I've spent a whole section on identity in this book.

2. Compassion (verse 12). Some versions translate "tenderhearted mercy" as "compassion." One of Merriam-Webster's definitions of mercy is "compassionate treatment of those in distress."[2] When the Bible says Jesus was moved with compassion, the literal translation is "moved in His bowels." That means feeling God's kind of love in your gut, your deepest soul, your innermost being. Compassion is seeing exactly where another person finds themselves and feeling moved in a deep way towards them.

3. Kindness (verse 12). Simply being kind is so underrated. Showing respect towards a person just because they are made in the image of God can make such an impact. You don't have to agree with them. But smile. Make eye contact. Be polite. Do something to help someone else, whether or not they deserve it.

4. Humility (verse 12). Rick Warren wrote, "Humility is not thinking less of yourself; it is thinking of yourself less."[3] It is putting aside our views and choosing to take God's view of ourselves and the people we encounter.

5. Gentleness (verse 12). This does not mean letting people run over you. It means being aware of the level of sensitivity with which you approach people. My friend Julie is the best example of this I've encountered. She knows how to "speak the truth in love" (Ephesians 4:15). She will tell you like it is and offer correction if needed, but she does so in a way that lets you know she truly cares about you. Caring about others is really at the heart of gentleness.

6. Patience (verse 12). Deep breath. This is a tough one. But Galatians tells us that one of the evidences of the Holy Spirit's work in our lives is patience (Galatians 5:22–23). So we know that through the Holy Spirit's work, we can continue to grow in patience.

7. Forgiveness (verse 13). One thing I've learned about forgiveness is it's really more for me than the other person. Our hearts are too precious to carry around the weight of bitterness, grudges, and unforgiveness.

We must persevere in obeying God and following how He has called us to live our lives. More on these in future chapters, but for now: What will you choose to "put on" today?

....

PRACTICE PERSEVERANCE: Which of these areas is most difficult for you? Ask God to help you continue to grow in these areas so that your life will be clothed in Him.

[2] Found at https://www.merriam-webster.com/dictionary/mercy.
[3] Rick Warren, The Purpose-Driven Life (Zondervan, 2013), p. 148.

DAY 9

Choose to Say Yes

"Just as our bodies have many parts and each part has a special function, so it is with Christ's body. We are many parts of one body, and we all belong to each other."

ROMANS 12:4 (NLT)

*H*ave you ever done something that you looked back on and thought, *Why did I do that?*

Several years ago, I was over at a friend's house on a Saturday helping them move into a new house. The wife offered for me to stay and have lunch, but I said no. I mumbled some excuse about needing to get home—even though I had nothing better to do.

My reasoning? I didn't want to "bother" them. At first, this sounds like a very humble and thoughtful response. It wasn't. It was really just insecurity on my part, fearing that I didn't belong—and I didn't want to stick around for that fear to be confirmed.

This was the lie I believed: I thought I wouldn't fit in. Nothing could have been further from the truth. This is one family that always accepts me with open arms and loves me even with all my quirks.

I lived for years turning down invitations to lunch or coffee or just to hang out with friends—all because I didn't know what to expect, so I'd rather not participate at all.

This particular Saturday has stayed in my mind. But instead of beating myself up over it, I decided to learn from it. After that day, I decided to never again make a decision like that out of fear. I made a private rule for myself: If someone invites me to lunch or just to hang out, I will say yes as much as I can. I can't always say yes, but I try to as much as possible. I also try to intentionally invite someone for coffee or lunch at least once a month.

Why?

Because I choose to be seen.

I choose to believe that I matter and my presence is a gift to others.

I choose to be a part of people's lives—even in the midst of everyday messiness.

I choose to invest time into friendships that are precious to me.

I choose to meet new people even when it's awkward.

I choose to step into the unknown for the sake of people's hearts.

It's good for me, and it's good for the people I choose to spend time with.

It takes practice learning to give the gift of your own presence, and it takes practice learning to receive what others have to offer. This requires perseverance. It means making the choice over and over again to say yes to the truth, yes to good friends, and yes to life.

So what will you choose?

PRACTICE PERSEVERANCE: Choose to say yes to healthy relationships with others. Schedule a lunch or coffee or play date with someone this week.

DAY 10

Masterpiece

"For we are God's masterpiece. He has created us anew in Christ Jesus, so we can do the good things He planned for us long ago."

EPHESIANS 2:10 (NLT)

J stood looking at myself in the mirror for the first time in months. My eyes still went critically over every physical flaw my mind told me I had. But I was getting tired of the tape that kept playing in my head. I knew what I thought about myself wasn't true, and I wanted the taunting inside me to stop. I surprised myself that day, because usually I avoided looking whenever I passed a mirror.

I had been struggling for several years with not liking my physical body. I didn't like my personality or the way I looked, and so finally I simply stopped looking at myself in the mirror. Of course, I would look in the mirror to put makeup on or fix my hair, but when I was getting ready for a shower or getting dressed for the day, I would scurry past the mirror with my head down, eyes averted.

That summer of my sophomore year in college, everything came to a head. I had been trying to take better care of myself, but I still struggled constantly with lies about being ugly or gaining weight. I remember sitting on my bed listening to Beth Moore's audio teaching "The LORD God Made a Woman"[4] for probably the fifth time. That message spoke the truth of God's Word to my heart, but I was struggling to fully grasp it.

It was time to shower and get ready for the day, but I was already cringing at the idea of walking past the mirror. Something had to change. I leaned my head back against the wall. "God," I prayed, "would You please help me to really believe the truth about myself, and see myself the way You see me?" I sat there for a few minutes in silence, then got up and headed for the shower.

As I walked into the bathroom, I looked at myself in the mirror. I heard God speak to my heart very clearly. It was not audible, but I knew God's thoughts were being reflected through my own mind at that moment, because I knew what I had previously been believing about myself. "You are a masterpiece," He said. "I am the one who created you, and only the one who creates something gets to say if it's truly beautiful."

I took a deep breath. And I chose to believe Him.

In that moment, God began to change the way I saw myself. It still took time and intentionality, and I still have to battle with the lies sometimes. But my mindset shifted, and I began to see myself as the masterpiece God says I am. Not just accepting my physical body, but also learning to accept the way God created my personality and relational traits.

Now, before you brush off this story and say that your body looks different than mine, or I don't know your situation—you're right. Your story and my story are different. Your body type and mine are different. But the truth of what God says about who we are is the same. It will take the daily choice of believing Him to change our mindsets and hearts. It may not happen overnight, but we can continue persevering by choosing to remember God's truth each day.

When God says we are His masterpieces, that does not just include our body types or physical appearance. God is telling you as His daughter that He created you, and because He created you—whatever your shape or size—God thinks you are incredible. God thinks you are beautiful. God thinks you are valuable and precious and worthy.

His opinion does not change. Our only choice is this: *Will we believe it?*

PRACTICE PERSEVERANCE: Do you believe you are a beautiful masterpiece? If not, ask God to help you see yourself the way He sees you. Choose to believe this truth today, my friend.

[4] Found at https://store.lproof.org/the-lord-god-made-a-woman.html.

DAY 11

Choose This Day

"Now therefore fear the Lord and serve him in sincerity and in faithfulness. Put away the gods that your fathers served beyond the River and in Egypt, and serve the Lord. And if it is evil in your eyes to serve the Lord, choose this day whom you will serve, whether the gods your fathers served in the region beyond the River, or the gods of the Amorites in whose land you dwell. But as for me and my house, we will serve the Lord."

(JOSHUA 24:14-15, ESV)

Joshua was the leader of the people of Israel after Moses passed away. They were about to exit the desert and step into the land that God promised them. But after all their years of living as slaves in Egypt, they had picked up a few of the local customs and habits, including the worship of multiple gods. Before they stepped into the promised land, Joshua gave them a choice: Either go back to their old ways of living and worshipping other gods, or choose to worship the one true God only and step into His promises.

We have been given that same choice. Will we choose to go back into the slavery of fear and lies? *You will never measure up. You're not good enough. You don't have what it takes. You are weak.* Or will we choose to step into all the promises of who God says we are?

I am chosen.

I am highly favored.

I have been given everything I need.

I am dearly loved.

I am adopted into God's family.

"So you have not received a spirit that makes you fearful slaves. Instead, you received God's Spirit when He adopted you as His own children" (Romans

8:15, NLT). Each day is a fight. It's true—every single day, we have to choose whose voice we listen to. It will take perseverance to make the right choice day after day, but it can be done. In fact, it must be done, not just for our own sakes but for others as well. Because what we believe about ourselves will have a ripple effect on how we see our situations and others around us. When we believe lies, we are critical of ourselves, which in turn means we are critical and jealous of others. But when we are secure and confident in who God says we are, we can accept ourselves (flaws and all). And we can cheer others on as well.

PRACTICE PERSEVERANCE: What will you choose today? How will you choose to apply the truth that you are an adopted child of God, and step into the promises He has laid in front of you?

PERSEVERING
in Prayer

"By definition, praying hard is hard because it's hard. But it's the prayers you pray when you feel like you want to quit praying that can bring the greatest breakthroughs."

MARK BATTERSON, *DRAW THE CIRCLE*

DAY 12

Fighting in Prayer

"Pray in the Spirit at all times and on every occasion. Stay
alert and be persistent in your prayers for all believers
everywhere. And pray for me, too. Ask God to give me the
right words so I can boldly explain God's mysterious plan
that the Good News is for Jews and Gentiles alike."

EPHESIANS 6:18–19 (NLT)

C. S. Lewis said, "Since it is so likely that children will meet cruel enemies, let them at least have heard of brave knights and heroic courage."

As part of a women's prayer group, I remember reading through Mark Batterson's *Draw the Circle*, a 40-day prayer journey. It was life-changing, challenging, and inspiring. Each of us started learning to "circle" specific things in our lives through prayer. We learned to pray God's Word over our situations. We also learned to pray for each other, especially when we encounter resistance—because, of course, Satan does not want us winning in this area of prayer.

When we pray, we will face struggles, because we have an enemy in the spiritual realm who opposes everything God wants to do. But God has given us weapons to fight and win. In 2 Corinthians 10:3–5, the Apostle Paul tells us, "We are human, but we don't wage war as humans do. We use God's mighty weapons, not worldly weapons, to knock down the strongholds of human reasoning and to destroy false arguments. We destroy every proud obstacle that keeps people from knowing God."

There comes a time even now when we must fight. Sometimes it's for ourselves and sometimes it's for others. We fight for our families, we fight for our friends, we fight for our churches.

This is not in the physical realm; it is spiritual, but that doesn't make it any less important.

We fight to choose life every day.

We fight in worship.

We fight in prayer.

We fight in faith.

There is an account in the book of Exodus when the Israelites were fighting a battle, and their leader, Moses, was standing at the top of the hill. Whenever he lifted his hands up, the Israelites were winning, but when he lowered them, the enemy began winning. Moses was very old at this time, and his hands grew tired. Two of the leaders had to hold up Moses' hands on either side, and the victory was won.

Our prayers matter. Just like those leaders with Moses, we are lending our strengths to others and speaking life over them when we pray for them. We are reminding them and ourselves of the truth of God's Word and speaking it into our reality on earth.

This does not mean we let our hearts get hard and bitter. We are willing to step out in courage—to step up and fight—because our hearts are tender, we care about people, and we are willing to fight for them in prayer (and in action, too).

This takes perseverance. These are not scared prayers. We are declaring God's Word over people and circumstances. We are reminding our own hearts that God is bigger than anything we might face. We do not fight as if we are ignorant of who will win the battle. We fight because we know our God is on our side, and He is victorious. He does not slumber or sleep, but will keep our hearts and lives safe—hidden in Him.

In the physical realm, this may or may not work out like we want. But we know we can trust our God and press hard into Him no matter what.

So fight, my friends. Fight in prayer.

* Fight for God's promises over your family
* over your work
* over your finances
* over your relationships
* over your life

Fight, and continue to fight—don't give up. Persevere.

PRACTICE PERSEVERANCE: Ask people to join you in prayer. Don't go into battle alone. Fight for each other in prayer and watch God do amazing things—*beyond anything you could ask or imagine.*

DAY 13

Unusual Battle Plans

"And Moses said to the people, 'Fear not, stand firm, and see
the salvation of the Lord, which he will work for you today....
The Lord will fight for you, and you have only to be silent.'"

EXODUS 14:13–14 (ESV)

In the Bible, God has a habit of using unusual battle plans. For instance, when Moses gave the above instructions to the Israelites, they had just left their slave masters in Egypt and were standing against the edge of the Red Sea. At that moment, their masters were charging in on chariots behind them, having decided they didn't want their slaves to leave after all.

Trapped, the Israelites were furious at Moses and cried, "Is this why you brought us all the way out here? To die?" Then the Lord said to Moses, "Tell the people of Israel to go forward" (v. 15). You are probably familiar with what happened next: Moses stepped into the water, stretched out his staff, and the waters parted wide enough for two million former slaves to cross over on dry ground. Then, as the Egyptians charged after them, the waters collapsed, drowning all their captors.

The people of Israel thought they were done. They thought for sure there was no way out. But God had a plan. It was just different than anything they could imagine.

Forty years later, when the Israelites were about to step out of the desert into the land God had promised, into conquering the first city of Jericho, their new leader Joshua was given similar instructions. (In case you missed it, the reason it took them 40 years to come into the promised land was because they kept choosing to disobey God, so they literally wandered in circles in the desert for 40 years until a new generation of believing people grew up and were ready to take the land. That could be a whole sermon right there. In fact, it probably is somewhere.)

Sally Lloyd-Jones wrote *The Jesus Storybook Bible*, which retells stories from the Bible, showing that all of God's Word points to Jesus and His rescue of us on the cross. I love how she describes this part of the Jericho story:

> *The people looked at Jericho. At the big, giant, scary walls around it…. What would they do? No one knew. But God knew…. So Joshua gathered his army together. They had their swords and spears and shields. They were ready to fight. But the plan wasn't about fighting; it was about trusting and doing what God said.* [5]

When we pray, we are trusting and doing what God says. And we are fighting—but in a different way. That day at Jericho, the whole army was dressed for battle. But they battled differently than expected. In a similar way, God calls us to battle in unexpected ways. He calls us to fight in prayer. As we read yesterday, fighting in prayer takes perseverance. We may feel weak, but He is strong, and He is victorious. He is powerful, and His name is greater than any other name. Prayer is not a passive activity. Prayer is *powerful*. So keep choosing to persevere in your prayers.

PRACTICE PERSEVERANCE: What part of your life needs some powerful prayer intervention right now? Start battling in prayer today by declaring who God is: "God, You are strong and You are always victorious. You are enough, and I know Your name is above every name. Would You come right now and show me how powerful You are in this situation? Thank You, God."

---

[5] Sally Lloyd-Jones, *The Jesus Storybook Bible*, Zonderkids 2007, p. 111.

DAY 14

Praying God's Word

"I pray for you constantly, asking God, the glorious Father
of our Lord Jesus Christ, to give you spiritual wisdom and
insight so that you might grow in your knowledge of God. I
pray that your hearts will be flooded with light so that you can
understand the confident hope He has given to those He called—
His holy people who are His rich and glorious inheritance."

EPHESIANS 1:16–18 (NLT)

When I was in college, I had the privilege of joining a women's prayer group. This was one of many groups that meet every week to pray for our church (even to this day). When I first started going, I was hesitant because I did not like praying out loud much. But as I listened to these women pray, I learned so much and gained confidence to practice it myself.

What did I learn? First of all, I noticed that these women almost always started their prayers by expressing thankfulness. They thanked God for who He is (because He doesn't change), and then they thanked Him for His promises and His faithfulness to do what He's promised. I noticed they would often pray Scripture. They would literally open up their Bibles and read out loud a verse or a chapter God was leading them to, and then speak that over whichever person or situation we were praying for at the moment.

I saw this pattern emerge over and over again, and I started trying it myself. Before this, most of my prayers were "help me" prayers or "please give me this" prayers. And while I do believe God wants us to tell Him what is going on in our lives and ask for things, this new form of praying unlocked a whole new world for me. Now when I pray, I try to start it off with thanking

God for who He is (this comes from the Bible, too) and focus on Him for a few minutes. This may sound something like: "God, thank You that You are my Shepherd, and because of that I have everything I need. Thank You that You lead me in places of peace; because You are right beside me, I will not be afraid. Thank you that Your goodness and Your love pursue me every single day of my life."

This method of prayer redirects my mind and heart; whatever has been bothering me or stressing me out takes a back seat. After I have spent some time worshipping and declaring who God is, then I can bring my concerns before Him and pray about what I need. But I do so with my heart changed. I am no longer panicking; my heart is strengthened in the truth of who God is and what His Word says.

As we've seen the last few days, prayer is powerful. You don't have to do it perfectly or have the right words. In fact, one of the most powerful things you can do is pray straight out of the Bible, because those are the words of God. It is so comforting for me to know that what I am speaking from God's Word is aligned with what God is doing. We don't try to come up with the magic words to get God to do what we want Him to do. We're just agreeing and speaking back to Him what He has already said! Let's persevere in prayer today by speaking out with God's Word.

PRACTICE PERSEVERANCE: Pick a verse or group of verses from the Bible that has meant something special to you recently, and practice praying them out loud—personalizing the verses to you and your situation as needed. If you need help knowing where to start, go to the Psalms; these are prayers already written down, so they're easy to apply personally.

DAY 15

Singing God's Word

"But I will sing of Your strength; I will sing aloud of Your
steadfast love in the morning. For You have been to me
a fortress and a refuge in the day of my distress."

PSALM 59:16 (ESV)

When I was growing up, my family had a group of CDs with many different Bible passages set to music. My sisters and I would play these children's songs over and over, but I'm not sure we knew we were literally singing God's Word.

One way to pray is to put our words to song. There have been many times when I felt too overwhelmed or tired, and I didn't know what to pray. But there are many talented people out there who have put the Bible into songs. For example, how many songs can you think of based on Psalm 23, the "Lord is my Shepherd" passage? Probably several. Once when I was in high school, our church youth group was working on a challenge to memorize Scripture verses, and my teammate and I figured out that you could sing Ephesians 4:32 to the tune of London Bridge. Go ahead and try it: "Be kind and compassionate to one another, forgiving each other, just as in Christ, God forgave you, Ephesians 4:32."

Acts 16 tells the story of church leaders Paul and Silas who were put in jail after performing a miracle. Paul freed a slave girl from an evil spirit in the name of Jesus, and the rich man who owned the slave girl could no longer earn money because the evil spirit that had enabled her to tell fortunes was now gone. The orders were given for Paul and Silas' ankles and hands to be bound with chains and they were put in stocks. Verse 25 says, "Around midnight Paul and Silas were praying and singing hymns to God, and the other prisoners were listening. Suddenly, there was a massive earthquake, and the prison was shaken to its foundations. All the doors immediately flew open, and the chains of every prisoner fell off!"

The Old Testament psalmist King David wrote prayers that he put into songs. One of those songs said this: "Though the cords of the wicked ensnare me, I do not forget Your law. At midnight I rise to praise You..." (Psalm 119:61–62, ESV).

Paul and Silas were not singing because they were happy to be in jail. They would have known this psalm; it would have been part of their training as Jewish young boys growing up. In this moment, they remembered King David's words. Here they were, in chains, bloody from being whipped, and in pain, but they made the choice to be obedient and sing to the Lord anyway. And God worked a miracle!

There are days when I'm worried or anxious and I have a hard time praying, but I can turn on a song that declares the goodness of God, that He has overcome, and that He loves me. How do I know these words to be true? They are right in the Bible.

- ◆ "You are good, and do only good." (Psalm 119:68, NLT)
- ◆ "I have told you all this so that you may have peace in Me. Here on earth you will have many trials and sorrows. But take heart, because I have overcome the world." (John 16:33)
- ◆ "For the Lord your God is living among you. He is a mighty savior. He will take delight in you with gladness. With His love, He will calm all your fears. He will rejoice over you with joyful songs." (Zephaniah 3:17)

See, God sings to you, so why shouldn't you sing back to Him?!

Pray God's Word and sing God's Word. This is my challenge for you today when it comes to persevering in prayer. You don't have to be perfect. You don't have to do it "correctly." But God's Word is powerful, and so is prayer. Put them together, and you've got an explosion that could rip open the heavens!

PRACTICE PERSEVERANCE: Find a song that declares who God is and what He has done, as He shows us in the Bible. Listen to it and sing it out loud as your prayer today!

DAY 16

Your Prayer Matters

"And when they had prayed, the place in which
they were gathered together was shaken, and they
were all filled with the Holy Spirit and continued
to speak the word of God with boldness."

ACTS 4:31 (ESV)

*J*f you've ever taken a trip to Nashville, you've probably been downtown
to Centennial Park. If you haven't been there, let me set it up for you. In
Centennial Park, there is a beautiful lake and a walking trail with trees,
plus these really cool free-standing swings with attached foot rests. Also in
this park is a *full-scale replica* of the Parthenon—a multi-pillared temple from
Athens, Greece, that houses a statue of the goddess Athena. (And yes, in this
full-scale replica of the Parthenon is a full-scale replica of the Athena statue.
I have never seen anything so huge in my entire life).

After first visiting and touring this attraction, I took time to walk along
the surrounding pathways, enjoying the nice weather and still in awe of this
enormous work of art. Centennial Park is in the middle of a neighborhood,
so I noticed moms pushing their kids on swings in their front yards. On
the grassy expanses of the park, a father and son were tossing a football.
They were acting like it was just another day at the park. All the while, right
behind them was this massive structure towering over the landscape. The
Parthenon.

I think prayer is like that sometimes. We get so used to our "everyday"
prayers: prayers before meals or prayers at church or prayers during our

Bible reading. But what we don't realize is that our prayers connect us to the one true God who is *massive*. Our prayers have the power to move mountains, because our prayers tap into the very heart of God; we are able to speak *what God says* over situations and people. That is mind-blowing.

Prayer is meant to be ongoing conversation with God. But sometimes the "everyday" nature of prayer can lead us to forget the power of God we have access to. Perseverance calls us to keep praying no matter what.

So don't settle for the lie that your prayers don't matter. My friend, your prayers move heaven and earth. Praying doesn't have to be perfect; we don't have to use fancy words. We are speaking out what we want God to hear, and then declaring what He says back to us. It is simple. But it is also powerful.

PRACTICE PERSEVERANCE: Ask God to reveal to you how powerful your prayers can be. Ask Him to put boldness in you to speak out in prayer what *He* says.

DAY 17

Be Present

"Pray in the Spirit at all times and on every occasion. Stay alert and be persistent in your prayers for all believers everywhere."

EPHESIANS 6:18 (NLT)

J've heard it said that some of the best ideas come in the shower. Some people sing in the shower. Some people just relish the quiet away from tiny humans. It's a place with few distractions.

I've also found the shower to be a great place to pray.

Usually in the morning, I get up to fix hot tea and then spend some time reading God's Word, journaling, and praying. Then I practice a few minutes of yoga or other stretches, and go for a walk in my neighborhood. When I get back home, I read a chapter from whatever book I'm currently on and then jump into the shower. Although I don't do this every day, I've started using shower time before a busy day to focus my heart and mind. I ask God to help me be completely present with every person I will meet that day.

As a counselor, I have the opportunity of being in the middle of some difficult and confusing times in people's lives, and I don't want to take that for granted. I want to truly listen, be tuned in to what's really going on, and be able to hear what God wants to say to that person through me. This takes intentional, focused prayer. Sometimes, when people leave my office, I will say a quick prayer out loud right then: "God, You know what this person's going through. Would You come and meet them today? Bring Your comfort and encourage them through Your Holy Spirit." Then I go on with my day. Prayer doesn't have to be complicated. But it does have to be intentional.

What are some ways you can be intentional about praying—for yourself, your family, your circle of influence? Part of persevering in prayer means intentionally choosing every day to be obedient to God in this area. Find creative ways that work for you. If you have a long commute to work, maybe you can use some of that time to pray for your coworkers or a difficult situation you know is coming up. Maybe there is a specific song you can use to help you express your thoughts to God. Maybe you can use your time cleaning the house to speak God's peace over everyone who lives and comes into your home.

Then listen to what God wants to say. Sometimes He will put a specific verse on your heart for the person you're praying for. Sometimes He will gently correct you or help you see something you didn't before. It's like any conversation—it's a two-way street. When we pray, we need to be intentional to speak but also intentional to listen. That's how we can be present in any relationship, and that's how we can be present in prayer.

PRACTICE PERSEVERANCE: Decide on one new way you're going to be intentional about praying and listening to God. Try it for at least a week and report what you are learning on Facebook. (Add the tag #sacredtenacity.)

PERSEVERING
in Sickness

....

"When life is rosy, we may slide by with
knowing about Jesus, with imitating Him
and quoting Him and speaking of Him. But
only in suffering will we know Jesus."

JONI EARECKSON TADA

DAY 18

When It Hurts

"Behold, You delight in truth in the inward being, and You teach me wisdom in the secret heart. Purge me with hyssop, and I shall be clean; wash me, and I shall be whiter than snow. Let me hear joy and gladness; let the bones that You have broken rejoice."

(PSALM 51:6–8, ESV)

*H*yssop (pronounced HISS-up), mentioned in this verse, is a type of wild oregano plant that grows specifically in the Mediterranean region. It has now been used in many kinds of healthcare remedies such as throat sprays and other treatments. The thing about hyssop is this: it stings. A lot. I've used hyssop spray over the years. If I have a sore throat, for example, I will spray hyssop on it. And it burns so much. But it brings healing faster than anything else I've tried.

One thing the psalmist is implying here is that just because there is pain does not mean healing isn't happening.

Now, let me dispel a myth right up front. Some people think that sickness and suffering is caused by sin being present in a person's life. Taken in context, Psalm 51 is the repentant prayer of King David after he had purposefully disobeyed God, killed someone by executive order, and then tried to cover it up. Once he knew he couldn't hide his actions from God, he took responsibility and asked for forgiveness. This psalm is part of his crying out to God.

I don't know where you are in life right now. Maybe you are dealing with chronic illness. Or you have a child or loved one who is ill or in the hospital or battling cancer. Maybe you or someone you know struggles with mental health issues. And maybe you have been told by some (perhaps well-meaning but also incorrect) people that the illness could be a result of some kind of sin or disobedience toward God.

I am here to tell you that is not true. Sometimes God allows things to happen in our lives that we don't understand. Our God has good plans for us and wants to bless us. But because we live in an imperfect world tarnished by sin, sometimes life happens, such as illness and disease, and there is no explaining it. However, God *wants to use* these unexplainable things in our lives for His good. That doesn't mean the thing itself is good. But God can still use it for good.

For example, because of health reasons, I have been told by doctors it is not safe for me to have biological children. However, God has given me the gift of being able to love on other people's kids and be a part of many families' lives. I also plan to foster or adopt kids of my own in the future. So that doesn't mean that the health issues I have gone through are good things, or that there is no pain in them. There has been pain. There has been suffering. There has been grieving. But God still brings beauty from the ashes.

I have chosen to keep persevering and believing that God has good things for me, even when I can't always see it. Every day I put one foot in front of the other, choose to speak the truth of God's Word, and choose to believe that He is good. And you can do the same thing, my friend.

So please don't discount your pain. Be honest with God; He can take it. But also don't discount the beauty that God can miraculously bring from (and maybe because of) what you are walking through.

PRACTICE PERSEVERANCE: Is there an area of your life that is painful right now? Ask God to come bring His comfort to you. He is not repelled by your pain. He is very near to you. What are some ways you can see God bringing healing in the midst of your pain?

DAY 19

Look for the Helpers

"Jonathan, David's uncle, was a wise counselor to the king, a man of great insight, and a scribe. Jehiel the Hacmonite was responsible for teaching the king's sons. Ahithophel was the royal adviser. Hushai the Arkite was the king's friend."

(1 CHRONICLES 27:32-33, NLT)

*D*uring my first major hospital stay, a friend made a list of Bible verses personalized for me. She had been praying these verses over me. Afterwards, I decided to make a list of my own promises that God had been speaking to me. I kept these in my journal and would pull them out on the bad days as reminders of what God was speaking to my heart. The next time I had to go to the hospital again, my dad blew up this list to poster-size and hung it in my hospital room, where it covered almost the entire window. You couldn't miss it. Anyone who walked in the room would immediately have their eyes drawn to it. One day, a nurse came in and immediately said, "Yes and Amen! That's true! You keep believing that!" And she might have had a small hallelujah moment right there next to my bed. It made me smile.

Fred Rogers famously said that his mom told him as a kid when he saw scary things on television, to "look for the helpers." The nurse in my room that day—and many other nurses and doctors like her—was one of the helpers in my story. King David, in today's verse, also had many helpers.

This small verse in 1 Chronicles is easy to miss. This chapter details the divisions of the people of Israel in service to the temple and the king. There were priests and Levites, worshippers who prophesied on their instruments, gatekeepers, vineyard keepers, those who tended the soil, and leaders of the army. Then this verse. Take a pen and circle the different roles mentioned in the verse above. Counselor. Scribe. Teacher. Royal adviser. Friend.

No one would even know about these people unless they read these verses. But their roles were still important. Some of the most influential people in my life are far from famous. But their impact in my life is something I will forever be grateful for. Friends. Mothers. Sisters. Brothers. Pastors. Fathers. Counselors. Doctors. Nurses.

Who are the helpers in your story? These are the people who help you persevere. Even if you are in the darkest valley, there are helpers around you. They may have behind-the-scenes roles, but their care, kindness, and sacrifices are important.

PRACTICE PERSEVERANCE: Use the space on this page to write down the names of some of your helpers. As an optional step, write one of them a quick note or send them a text to say thank you.

DAY 20

Joy and Sadness

"I will never forget this awful time, as I grieve over my loss.
Yet I still dare to hope when I remember this: The faithful
love of the Lord never ends! His mercies never cease. Great is
His faithfulness; His mercies begin afresh each morning."

LAMENTATIONS 3:20-23 (NLT)

In 2015, Pixar released an animated movie called *Inside Out*. It may be an animated film, but I don't think it's just for kids. (If you haven't seen it, you need to watch it at least once—just my opinion!) In short, the movie highlights an eleven-year-old girl named Riley, and the five personified "emotions" that live inside of her brain. They follow Riley through the ups and downs of her life—including a big move away from her friends and into a new school.

Towards the end of the movie (spoiler alert!), Riley decides to not listen to anyone anymore, and she runs away from home. She shuts down her emotions and boards the city bus. It's here that the ringleader of Riley's brain, Joy, calls into action Sadness—an emotion who, up to this point, has only seemed to be a nuisance and a burden. But Joy realizes that Riley can't just be happy all the time. Sometimes she has to be sad. And that's not a bad thing. Riley returns to her parents and starts crying. She tells them she misses home. They hug her and tell her they miss home, too. In the midst of her deep sadness, Riley allows herself to be comforted by her parents, and a relieved smile comes to her face.

When I saw this scene of the movie for the first time, it seemed to put into words something I've never been able to express: Joy and sadness can be felt at the same time. We won't always be happy, but we won't always be sad, either. Sometimes we will have to hold the tension of sadness and grief at the same time as gratitude and joy. They are not mutually exclusive.

So if you are going through a difficult time in your life, don't try to push away your emotions. Learn to be okay with holding grief and gratefulness at the same time. You might need to talk with a counselor or a trusted friend to help sort it out. Your sadness and loneliness and pain are valid. Your blessings and moments of laughter are valid, too. One does not cancel out the other. Sometimes life just has both. But that's okay. "His mercies begin afresh each morning."

PRACTICE PERSEVERANCE: Are you going through something right now that has both joy and sadness, grief and gratefulness? Ask God to help you be okay with the tension of experiencing both, and to show you specifically how His mercies are new for you today. If you need help with this step, find a trusted friend or counselor to talk with. It's okay to ask for help.

DAY 21

Songs of Victory

"For You are my hiding place; You protect me from
trouble. You surround me with songs of victory."

PSALM 32:7 (NLT)

J woke up to the sound of music. A song was playing...a girl was singing...
Wait, that was *my* song! That was *my* voice! *How did they get my song?*
I wondered groggily.

Months before I ever was admitted into the hospital for emergency
surgery, I had given a copy of a song I had written to D'Ann, the wife of one
of my pastors. When she heard the news that I was in the hospital and might
not last through the night, D'Ann suddenly remembered the copy of the song
I had given her. She told me later she was up late that night scouring the
house for it. Finally, in the wee hours of the morning, she found the CD where
it had fallen behind the baker's rack in her kitchen. She sent it up to the
hospital with someone visiting and said, "She needs to hear this song. She
needs to hear her own voice speak life over herself."

Even though I was in a coma for another six days, this was one of the
songs that was constantly playing in my room's CD player. During this and
the following surgeries and recovery times, I learned to have worship music
going almost 24/7. Sometimes I was too tired to do anything but lay in my
bed and listen, letting the music wash over me. Other times, I would wake
up and realize the music had stopped, and I would start the playlist again

before I went back to sleep.

The power was not in the music; the power was in what the music welcomed. Even instrumental scores of worship songs are powerful, though no words are sung. Why? Because these songs welcome in the Holy Spirit. These songs declare the goodness of God and who He is. These songs were my prayers when I could not pray. They were my encouragement when I felt alone. They were my refreshing when I was too tired to move. Just like the psalmist says, God surrounds us with songs of victory, songs of deliverance, songs of hope.

You don't have to wait for a crisis to worship. Start today. Whatever you are facing today, turn on music that speaks out who God is and the truth of what He says about you. The songs you picked out on Day 15—play and sing these songs as declarations of God's Word into your day. Sacred tenacity in the Christian life involves choosing again and again to speak God's truth to ourselves; worship helps us do this. Worship invites God's presence to come. As Psalm 16:11 says, "In Your presence is fullness of joy." This doesn't mean everything's perfect. It doesn't mean we're always "happy." It means His presence is with us *wherever* we are, and we can have joy knowing that because of the Holy Spirit, we are not alone, we are strengthened, and we are loved.

PRACTICE PERSEVERANCE: Make a playlist of worship songs that declare who God is and the truth of who you are in Him. These declarations are true even when your circumstances may be terrible. Let God's truth through music invite God's presence into your day.

DAY 22

Above Every Name

"And being found in human form, He humbled Himself by becoming obedient to the point of death, even death on a cross. Therefore God has highly exalted Him and bestowed on Him the name that is above every name, so that at the name of Jesus every knee should bow, in heaven and on earth and under the earth, and every tongue confess that Jesus Christ is Lord, to the glory of God the Father."

PHILIPPIANS 2:8–11 (ESV)

Somewhere a heart monitor is beeping. I hear the whoosh of a ventilator. My eyes crack open. There is a large, sky blue curtain at the foot of the bed on which I'm lying; it's drawn open. I can see beyond the doorway a long counter, and hear the chatter of nurses beyond it at the nurses' station. My eyes drop down to the sheet covering my body. My hand is lying on top of the sheet, except it and my whole arm is wrapped completely in ace bandages.

I remember this moment in the hospital bed years ago almost every time I am worshipping at church. Why? Because often I come to church distracted or discouraged by something that's going on in my own life, and God brings this memory to my mind in order to remind me that He is bigger than my circumstances. "See?" He seems to whisper to my heart. "Remember that I saved your life? That means nothing is too big for Me. I am powerful and victorious. I fight on your behalf. And I will do it again. I saved your life for a reason. Declare what I have done. Nothing is too big for Me." Something deep inside me rises up in this moment, something I can't fully explain, and a determination rises up in me, like the psalmist wrote, "My soul *will* bless the Lord" (see Psalm 42:5).

Jesus came to earth in the skin of a human being. That means He knows what it's like to suffer in a world marred by sin and death and misery. But He rose up from the grave—meaning He is completely victorious over death and everything that it represents. Death holds no power over us any longer. Fear has no place in God's presence. Lies have no bearing in the light of God's victory. Jesus has been given the *name above every name*. That means every fear has to bow under the name of Jesus. Every sickness has to leave in the name of Jesus. Every lie is banished in the name of Jesus.

Unless we let them, death and sin and fear have no place in our lives as believers. *They have no real power.* When God reminds me in this memory of my time in the hospital, the Holy Spirit speaks to my heart: "I have brought victory over death. Whatever you face has to submit to Me. I am the name above every name. That means sickness; that means death; that means fear; that means troubles. They all have to come under Me, because I am greater."

In that moment, I choose to bow the knee and put whatever I'm struggling with at His feet. Because He is greater.

What does this mean in a world where clearly not all sickness or sin or death is gone? We have to choose to believe that God is still greater, even when we don't always see it. In an imperfect world, there will be suffering. But God wants to come alongside you through every pain. And even in the pain, we have a choice to say, "God, You are greater. Your name is above every name. Even when I don't understand, thank You that You are in control. Thank You that You see me, and You care for me, and You are with me no matter what."

This is not succumbing to helplessness. This is choosing to persevere. Yes, pray for supernatural healing to come. Pray for death and sickness to be defeated. So many people prayed for me during this hospital stay—people I don't even know. And while I wasn't instantly, miraculously healed—God used many good doctors to bring me to health over time—it was a miracle that I survived at all. Doctors told my family, "I don't know how she made it." Well, I do.

Healing may not look like you wanted; sometimes it takes different forms. But illness or grief or sickness does not define who you are. God's purpose for you is greater than this. Because He is not limited to what our eyes can see in this life. God's power is not limited by our limits or weaknesses. In fact, He often takes great pleasure in showing His strength through us just when we feel at our weakest.

PRACTICE PERSEVERANCE: What limits or weaknesses seem to define you? Choose today to put these things under God's strength and declare that His name is above every name. You can use the examples from this page to help you pray that out.

PERSEVERING
in Health

· ·

"I'm pretty sure that God, if He called me to
chat about my body, would say things like, 'I
like your body. I created your body, and if you
have read the first chapter of Genesis lately,
you might recall that I called Creation good.'"

LAUREN F. WINNER, *MUDHOUSE SABBATH*

DAY 23

Your Physical Health

"Dear friend, I hope all is well with you and that you
are as healthy in body as you are strong in spirit."

3 JOHN 1:2 (NLT)

When I was fifteen years old, I was diagnosed with an intestinal disease called ulcerative colitis. After trying to treat it with medicine to no avail, my parents decided to start managing my symptoms through a nutritionist. For the next year, I was on an extremely restricted diet. I learned some key things during this time about what foods my body can and can't handle, but (being a typical teenager) I did not have much internal self-motivation to keep eating properly. It was a struggle for me for many years following.

Due largely in part to these health issues and the restricted diet I'd had since high school, for a long time after I had a disordered way of looking at food. I always struggled with the irrational fear (though I didn't put words to it until years later) that if I didn't eat the food now, it would be taken away from me. Also, I began to worry about how food affected my weight. During my freshman and sophomore years of college, I would alternate between eating hardly anything during the day to wanting to eat everything in sight. I knew it wasn't good for me, but I didn't know how to stop.

Eventually I got brave enough to share with a trusted adult, and she helped walk me through the healing process over many months. I often called her when I was struggling. We would talk about my food habits, and she encouraged me to take care of my body in a healthy way. She explained that, at the moment, I was seeing food as bad. But food is neither good nor bad. "The enemy is wanting to take away your bread," she told me. In other words, Satan was using these lies and fears I was believing to get me to sabotage my eating habits, my physical body, and as a result, my life. "Don't you want to have the energy to do all the things you enjoy doing?" she asked me.

That was a starting point.

Over time, I learned to eat in a way that is healthy and helpful for my body. This took perseverance and tenacity, because every meal presented me with a choice. It was then I had to decide how I would treat my body. Would I put in the good "fuel" of healthy food, or would I deprive my body of much-needed nutrients?

The signals our body gives us (when we're full, when something messes with our "system," etc.) are from God. He has created our bodies in magnificent ways. We would do well to learn how to care for our bodies in the way they need to be cared for, so that we can be at our best and ready to go at whatever God puts in front of us to do. Staying aware of these signals will help us persevere in working for His kingdom.

Taking care of yourself is not selfish; it is healthy.

Your physical health has strong ties to your emotional and mental health as well. I've found that when I take care of my physical body in a healthy way (more vegetables, less sugar, moderate exercise), I can think clearer, I have more energy, and I am in a better mood. Our physical bodies and our spiritual bodies are connected; it makes no sense to take care of one but not take care of the other.

PRACTICE PERSEVERANCE: What area of your physical health do you need to work on the most? Write down a specific plan (how much, how many days a week) for one way you're going to take better care of your physical body. Take a moment to thank God today for creating your physical body and equipping you to do the things He has put in front of you to do.

DAY 24

Your Emotional Health

*"And let the peace that comes from Christ rule in
your hearts. For as members of one body you are
called to live in peace. And always be thankful."*

COLOSSIANS 3:15 (NLT)

*B*eing friends with people who have kids means I often go to the sports games of my friends' kids. This means I can sometimes be seen at a junior high basketball or volleyball game. Most recently, it was a Little Dribblers game. These are first graders. Let's face it: in first grade, most kids don't know how to play basketball. And even though they've been coached, sometimes they forget once they get on the court. (I may or may not have been this kid, too, when I was a first grader).

The team I've been watching has an excellent referee. She has fun with the kids, you can tell she loves basketball, and yet she still teaches them right in the middle of the game. The ref becomes less of a whistleblower and more of an additional coach.

"When you get the ball, you can't hold it in front of you and run. You have to dribble, like this."

"When the other team is throwing the ball in, move back to the other side of the court."

"Wait, let's stop and make sure your shoe is tied."

The Greek word for "rule" in today's verse means to discern or decide between, like a judge, or a referee at a game. "Let the peace of Christ [the inner calm of one who walks daily with Him] be the controlling factor in your hearts [deciding and settling questions that arise]" (Amplified version).

Someone once gave me some great advice: "Follow the peace." Jesus is called the Prince of Peace. One of the fruits (evidences) of the Holy Spirit is peace. Which begs the question: Are the choices you're making right now lining up with the peace of God in your heart? I'm not even talking about sin issues here. What about the daily choices that are part of your life right now? How are you practicing perseverance when it comes to allowing God's peace into your life?

Your emotional health will always affect your physical health. If I allow myself to get worried or stressed for days at a time, I start getting a knot in my stomach, and I don't eat or sleep very well.

We have to intentionally make room for peace. Here are a few practical ideas:

- Turn off your phone for a day.
- Turn on worship music.
- Turn off the TV for the weekend and spend time with family.
- Go for a walk without listening to music or a podcast; enjoy nature around you.
- Quit doing something you feel like you "should" do.
- Do something that refreshes you.

How will you choose to make room for God's peace in your life? "Let the peace of Christ rule in your hearts..." Let God's peace make the judgement call over what your mind and heart focus on today.

PRACTICE PERSEVERANCE: What is one step you will take to choose God's peace today? Ask God to help you surrender to Him, allowing Him to make the judgement calls over your heart and mind.

DAY 25

Stay Active

"She dresses herself with strength
and makes her arms strong."

PROVERBS 31:17 (ESV)

*P*lease don't skip today's practice. Talking about staying active is not meant to bring you a feeling of shame in any way. Let's just talk.

Each verse in Proverbs 31 is meant to encourage us, especially as women. The "Proverbs 31 Woman" is overwhelming to a lot of us because it seems like she has it all together—and by the way, does she even sleep?! But thanks to my friend D'Ann, I have come to see the woman in this chapter in a different light.

I've learned that each verse in Proverbs 31 sheds light on a different aspect of who we are as women: We need to first be confident in our value and who God says we are. Then we are able to be a support to those around us. We take care of our families and those entrusted to us. We are creative. We ask God to show us who needs us the most today, and we do our best to meet that need. We speak encouraging words. We work hard and make our homes beautiful.

Proverbs 31 is not meant to be a list of impossible tasks we will never measure up to. It is a beautiful picture of how God has gifted us as women to reach out to those in our homes and communities. It's meant as an encouragement.

In today's verse, the encouragement is that a woman of excellence "dresses herself with strength and makes her arms strong." What does this mean for us today? It means we do what we must to take care of our bodies. We exercise, we eat well, we stay active. This is going to look different for each of us. You may have young kids at home, and it is all you can do just to keep up with them—forget exercising at the gym! My question to you would be this: Do you feel physically fit enough to do what you need to do? I will say it again: Taking care of yourself is not selfish; it is healthy.

My sister is a runner. She's even completed a marathon and multiple half-marathons. I will never be a runner. It makes me hurt. But I do yoga and walk in my neighborhood almost every day.

What is something you can do to stay active and enjoy it? (Or at least learn to enjoy it?) Do that. Are you more of a group person? Maybe you could get together with some friends and do zumba or a spin class or ballroom dancing. Maybe you like to play tennis or basketball or ice skating. Maybe you'd rather be by yourself on a long hike or pumping it out on the weight machines or elliptical, or following an exercise video in your living room. Whatever is fun to you (or could become fun), do that thing.

Why is it important for us to talk about this? Because God has put dreams and callings in your heart that only you can do. And your physical body needs to be ready to do those things. If we don't take care of ourselves and our physical bodies are dragging behind, that's not being good stewards of what God has given us. I'm talking to myself here, too. Sometimes I'm not the greatest at doing what I need to do to take care of myself. It takes discipline and perseverance to get up when the alarm goes off, put on exercise clothes, and to stay active every day. But I'm learning that if I prepare myself physically, then I'm more ready mentally and spiritually for what God puts in front of me.

PRACTICE PERSEVERANCE: Make a plan for how you are going to start (or continue) to stay physically active—whatever that looks like for you. Ask God to prepare your physical body and your spiritual heart for the things He wants you to do.

DAY 26

Speak Kindly to Yourself

"Thank you for making me so wonderfully complex! Your workmanship is marvelous–how well I know it."

PSALM 139:14 (NLT)

Many days when my alarm goes off in the morning, I don't want to get out of bed to exercise. But one reason I choose to get up and go exercise several times a week is simple: *Because I can.* I know what it's like to learn to walk again after a septic infection ravaged my body. I know what it's like to have massive blood clots in my legs, which doctors said has only been seen in less than one percent of patients. But during recovery, as I began to slowly limp around my neighborhood, allowing my body to get stronger over time, I realized I get to exercise because I am alive and because I've been given this moment—and because I can.

I think of my young friend David, who I've known since he was three years old. He's a teenager now, and growing fast. When he was 5 months old, he suffered a stroke that resulted in significant weakness on the entire left side of his body. Over the years, David has worked hard to strengthen himself through physical therapy and continued practice. David is a go-getter who loves sports and being active, and he puts his heart fully into everything he does. He is a brave young man who maintains a positive attitude and doesn't let anything hold him back. I want to be brave and tenacious like David. *Because I can.*

As I've said before, our physical health affects our emotional, mental, and spiritual health. And we need to be physically prepared (as much as we can) to do what God has put in front of us. That takes perseverance. But in the midst of this, let me encourage you: Please speak kindly to yourself, and especially about your body. Even if your physical health is not where you want it to be right now, this is still the one body God has given you. Don't speak negatively about yourself. You are doing the best you can. And each day you get to choose to continue to do the best you can to the best of your ability.

What if you have a disability that keeps you from being what you think is the "best" version of yourself physically? What if you are in a wheelchair? What if you've had major surgery? What if you've just had a baby? What if you're recovering from chemo? What do you do then? *You do the best you can for today.* Don't compare yourself to other people.

Speak kindly to yourself and to your body. Physical fitness looks different for each person. You find what is the best version for you.

PRACTICE PERSEVERANCE: Ask God to show you what is the best way for you to take care of your physical body, in whatever season you find yourself. Make a commitment to speak kindly to yourself today.

DAY 27

The Value of Rest

> "I know the Lord is always with me. I will not be shaken,
> for He is right beside me. No wonder my heart is
> glad, and I rejoice. My body rests in safety."
>
> PSALM 16:8–9 (NLT)

*D*o you ever feel like there are not enough hours in your day? You know you can't keep going at this pace, but you don't know what you could leave out. All too often, what happens next is that the most important things get dropped first.

Earlier this year, I decided to take the majority of my Thursdays (since I'm self-employed) to take a "sabbath" rest. The meaning of this may be different than you think. John Mark Comer, in his book *Garden City*, puts it this way:

> *"Jesus does some of his best work on the Sabbath. Which is fitting. The Sabbath is all about intimacy with God. And healing is a sign of God's love for you. What better time for Jesus to heal than on the Sabbath?... We get tired in body and in soul. We need more than a twenty-four hour armistice from work; we need an encounter with Jesus' healing power."*[6]

The two questions Comer uses in his book as guidelines for taking a sabbath are 1) *Is it restful?* and 2) *Is it worship?*

I've come to see that this purposeful slowing of a sabbath rest is vital for my health—physically, spiritually, mentally, and emotionally. My schedule's getting crazier, and even though it's only from bedtime Wednesday to about 4pm on Thursday for now, I *need* this time to shut everything down and rest.

Rest is not the same as being lazy.

Rest does not necessarily mean "do nothing."

Rest means asking, *What is refreshing to my soul?* What makes you walk away inspired and encouraged and refreshed?

What does this look like? For me, it usually means taking a walk, eating dinner, FaceTime or a phone call with a friend, and reading a lot. No TV or social media (I do not come away from that rested). It's not about following rules. Only these two questions need to be asked: 1) Is it restful (for you)? 2) Is it worship?

Working in the garden may be restful for some, but not others. Going for a run may be invigorating for some, but not for others.

This will look differently if you have a house full of young kids. Maybe your spouse or a friend could keep them for a few hours, or you could take "shifts." For some families, you could find a fun activity to do outside together. Maybe it means going on a walk or riding bikes together. I heard of one mom putting spa face masks on everyone (kids included!), turning the lights down, and telling them *we're all going to play the quiet game now.*

Whatever it looks like for you, find a block of time that you schedule every week to spend time letting your body and soul recharge. You need it. I need it. We need rest in order to persevere in our calling and work. Life is not a sprint; it is a marathon. Your work, your family, your health, and your life will be better when you choose every week to step back from the chaos and choose to rest.

PRACTICE PERSEVERANCE: Pull out your calendar and schedule a few hours of rest for every week this month. Have the courage to stick to it, but also be flexible with how intentional rest is going to look like in your life. Ask God to heal you and refresh you with His Holy Spirit during this time.

[6] John Mark Comer, *Garden City* (Zondervan, 2017), p. 228, 233).

PERSEVERING
in Disappointment

"Every time we're faced with the unexpected, we have the choice to embrace it wholeheartedly or halfheartedly. Embracing it wholeheartedly keeps us moving forward in life; embracing it halfheartedly keeps us from growing."

CHRISTINE CAINE, *UNEXPECTED*

DAY 28

Acknowledge the Loss

"I could ask the darkness to hide me and the light
around me to become night–but even in darkness I
cannot hide from You. To You the night shines as bright
as day. Darkness and light are the same to You."

PSALM 139:11-12 (NLT)

bout a year ago, one of my very best friends moved away. She
moved across state lines with her husband to an amazing job in a
place where their daughter can run and play and laugh and explore,
and where they truly feel peaceful. When they moved, I was happy for them,
because I knew this was where God had led them. But there was still a part
of me that grieved the change as a kind of loss. Because it was a loss. And
it's okay to experience loss—that's being human.

What loss or disappointment are you facing right now? Maybe you have
lost a job, or didn't get that promotion you thought you would. A relationship
could be really hard right now. A relationship didn't work out. An adoption
fell through.

Even positive change (like marriage or a job promotion or a new baby)
brings a sense of stress, because our brains and emotions are trying to
figure out how to deal with all that comes as part of this new territory. I
don't know about you, but sometimes I have to remind myself that I have
an adult brain, and I can learn to deal with change in a mature way. We all
know that changes are inevitable, but very few of us know how to handle
change well.

So what are some ways we can learn to do this? Here are three ways I've found to be helpful:

- **Acknowledge the change.** Whether the change is good or not so good, it can't be ignored. Don't suppress the emotions that come up; share them with someone. If it's a new job, there is going to be a learning curve, and that's okay. If you just lost a family member, there are going to be days you cry for no reason. That's okay. If you just adopted a child, there are going to be sleepless nights and months of truly getting to know each other and building trust. That's okay. Say it out loud, and embrace the change for what it is.
- **Let others help.** Find trusted people who can be with you during this time. Whether it's asking someone to go on a walk with so you don't have to be alone, or calling someone to watch your kids because you just need one hour alone—let other people live life with you.
- **Find a "new normal."** This might take a while. Change means things will not be the same as before. That is okay. Life is always changing. Give yourself permission to find a new normal. Discover new routines and new little blessings that make you smile in this emerging season. Learn to settle into how things are now, instead of always pining for how things used to be. Remember the good things from before *and* embrace the great things to come!

Keep persevering, my friend. It will be worth it!

PRACTICE PERSEVERANCE: Spend a moment thanking God that He is with you even when things around you are changing. If you are in the middle of a loss or change, tell Him how you feel about it, and ask His comfort and peace to surround you today.

DAY 29

Don't Compare Pain

"[Hannah] replied. '...I am very discouraged, and I
was pouring out my heart to the Lord...For I have
been praying out of great anguish and sorrow.'"

I SAMUEL 1:15–16 (NLT)

y maternal grandmother struggled with Alzheimer's for several
years. It was very hard on my grandad, too, in caring for her. I
remember after one particularly difficult weekend visiting them, I
shared with my friend D'Ann how sad it made me to watch them slip away.
I tried to brush off the emotions rising in me. "But I know that everyone has
to go through this with their grandparents," I added.

She stopped me there. "Don't compare pain with pain," she told me. She
explained that I shouldn't minimize what I'm struggling with. Every person
with grandparents has to go through the process of saying goodbye, but
that does not make my own loss any less important. I shouldn't compare
someone else's pain with my own pain. What was causing me pain was
big to me, and that's all that mattered. It's important to me, and it's valid
to grieve.

She explained to me the value of "holding my grief." I need to be honest
about my feelings and be willing to hold them and be with them just as they
are. And then I can begin to allow God to take these feelings and speak to
me about them and heal me. But I can't rush the process. I have to start
being okay with holding the pain. This may mean learning to hold the pain in

the presence of a trusted counselor or friend. But if we deny or run from the pain, we won't be able to eventually release it and receive healing.

Today's verse comes from Hannah, a woman who experienced lots of pain, loss, and trouble. She lived in a culture that saw bearing children as a sign of God's blessing, yet she was barren. Her husband had two wives (also a fairly accepted practice at that time), and the other wife had many children. To make matters worse, this wife taunted Hannah constantly about it. So Hannah found refuge in the temple and poured her heart out to God. She did not try to hide her pain or pretend it wasn't there. She was honest with God and (as the rest of the chapter shows) with the temple priest, Eli. At first Eli didn't believe her, but he ended up prophesying to her about the son that would be coming to her.

God heard this woman's prayers. He was not afraid of or put off by her sorrow and discouragement. Instead, He used it to show his blessing in the most beautiful way. God is not afraid of your pain, either. He can take whatever you have. He wants to hold it with you. Being honest about our pain and being willing to receive healing will take perseverance. How His blessing comes may not be on our timetable, and it most likely won't look like we expected. But He is still faithful, He still wants us to come to Him, and He still answers our prayers.

PRACTICE PERSEVERANCE: What things are causing you sorrow or anguish today? Are you willing to hold your pain before God and let him bring His comfort? Ask God for what you need today.

DAY 30

Grief Has No Time Limit

"He heals the brokenhearted and bandages their wounds.
He counts the stars and calls them all by name."

PSALM 147:3–4 (NLT)

$\mathcal{T}$here are still times when I miss my maternal grandparents so much it brings me to tears. I have friends who lost precious family members years ago, yet they still have moments of sadness and deeply missing their loved ones. That's because there is no time limit to grief. True, the passing of time may help ease the wound, but the loss of someone will never heal completely on this side of heaven.

Have you ever lost someone? A spouse? A child? A potential adoption? A stillborn infant? A precious friend? Take the time you need to grieve. Grief comes in waves; it is unpredictable. Some days you may be finding your "new normal," and other days you may barely be functioning. That is completely okay. That is part of the process of grief, however painful it may be. Be willing to persevere and give yourself the space and the permission to grieve how you need to. In this space, God will begin to bind up your wounds. He sees you and He knows exactly what you're going through. He is with you and has not forgotten you. Author Emily P. Freeman writes, "Grief does deep, important, and sacred work."[7]

Today's verse notes, "He counts the stars and calls them all by name." Think about it: There are billions of stars in the night sky, and yet our God knows each and every one of them by name. He knows your name, too. And He cares for you, especially in your times of greatest sorrow. Allow this time to do its deep work in you. Let God pull you in close. Don't rush it. In John 11, when some of Jesus' dearest friends lost their brother, He wept with them. He is not afraid of your pain.

One of the most difficult things about grief is that you have no way to plan for what happens next. The season following the initial loss is full of the unexpected. You've never been here before, and you're not sure what to do. That's okay. This, too, is normal. Allow God and other trusted people around you to guide you and help walk you through this season.

In a little book called *Mudhouse Sabbath*, Lauren F. Winner references Jewish traditions and parallels their practices to everyday (non-Jewish) life. About the mourning process, she says this:

> *The mourner who wants to weep in his cups alone is out of luck. On those days when he desires nothing more than to crawl back under the covers and shut out everything that breathes and has three dimensions, people pack into his home...[He prays] not alone in his den but there in the community of God's faithful.* [8]

Can I challenge you? Let people into your pain. The people who you've built trust with. Let them know what you're feeling and how you are struggling. Let them hug you and help you and send food to you and pray with you. Even when you want to say no—and want to try to hold it all together—choose to say yes.

On the hard days, the introvert in me almost wants to just go home and be in silence. But I need to be around those I trust, too. I need to know I am not alone. I need to sit side by side with people, as I simultaneously mourn and remember the good things. So I go for a walk. I invite someone for coffee or tea. I pick up the phone and call a friend. And in this, the people around me become a tangible representation of the God who will always be there for me.

PRACTICE PERSEVERANCE: Are you in a season of grieving right now? What are some ways you remember the good even in the midst of grieving? Who can you choose to let into your life today?

[7] Freeman, *A Million Little Ways* (Revell, 2013), p. 117.

[8] Lauren F. Winner, *Mudhouse Sabbath* (Paraclete Press, 2007), p. 34–35.

DAY 31

Lift Up Your Eyes

"Look up into the heavens. Who created all the stars?
He brings them out like an army, one after another,
calling each by its name. Because of His great power and
incomparable strength, not a single one is missing. O Jacob,
how can you say the Lord does not see your troubles?
O Israel, how can you say God ignores your rights?"

ISAIAH 40:26–27 (NLT)

J am so grateful for the group of ladies I get to pray with every week. This group of women gathers to pray for our church, pastors, and leaders. But we also pray for each other, especially if one of us is struggling with a difficult life situation. These women inspire me with their passion, encourage me with their vulnerability, and strengthen me with their prayers. Collectively, this group of women (past and present) have been through every joy and sorrow imaginable. We've celebrated miracles and mourned great losses. But we keep choosing to show up, intercede, and declare what God is doing in our church, our hearts, and our region.

God put people around us for a reason. We were made to live life in community. Who are the people God has put around you? Where are the families God has called you to connect with? Who are the ones He is prompting you to serve? The wife of one of my pastors once told me that when she is feeling discouraged or depressed, she has found that serving someone else lifts her up more than anything. Perhaps God is calling you to step outside your own disappointments today and show kindness to someone around you.

This does not mean what you are going through is not important. God sees your pain. But He also knows the treasure of His Spirit that He's put inside you, and maybe He's prompting you to share this gift with others today. This requires perseverance because it means thinking outside of your own desires and needs in the midst of a difficult time. Lift up your eyes. Who around you is also hurting? Maybe you could write them a note. Bring them a meal. Share a word of encouragement.

God holds all the stars. And He also holds the hearts of every single one of His children. Just because He's prompting you to reach out to someone else's heart does not mean He is abandoning yours. On the contrary: "Those who refresh others will themselves be refreshed" (Proverbs 11:25, NLT).

PRACTICE PERSEVERANCE: Thank God that He holds your heart and knows you by name. Ask Him to show you whose heart needs encouragement and a kind touch today.

DAY 32

Embrace This Season

"The Lord God placed the man in the Garden
of Eden to tend and watch over it."

GENESIS 2:15 (NLT)

Almost every culture on earth has a creation story. But the story of the Creator God in Genesis is different from all others.

In most cultures, the story goes something like this: The gods who were in charge of the universe got tired of doing work on Earth. It was hard and loathsome, and they were worn out. So they decided to make human beings to be their workers, to slave over the earth, so that they could live blissful lives as deities being served by the little humans.

In John Mark Comer's book *Garden City*, he points out the main difference in the biblical creation story, which should affect our view of our own work every day. In the Bible's account, God created man in *His own image*, to be a co-creator with Him—to partner with Him in working the garden, taking care of the animals, and enjoying all the good things.

Did you get that? We are partners with God in His world. We are not His slaves. He has put creativity and motivation and ideas in us for a reason. We are called to build, create, expand, and improve our world—because that is the heart of God.

In the same way, what each of us does for our work should be done in such a way that it brings God's kingdom and His ways into our world.

- During the spring months, I am very grateful for my tax accountant. When she takes time to answer my questions, treats me kindly, and files my taxes with excellence, this woman brings God's kingdom into my life.
- If you are a graphic designer, be a really good graphic designer. Your work is good, and it is bringing God's kingdom to earth.
- If you are a mom, love on your kids and raise them the best you can, because you are bringing heaven into your house and the lives of your little ones.
- If you are a teacher, be the best teacher you can be. Even when you don't see the results immediately, your work is bringing God's ways and His kingdom into the lives of everyone you come into contact with.

Embrace the season you are in. Don't wish it away. Your work is good. It is not meant to be burdensome. It is meant to bring heaven to earth. So keep persevering in your work, even when it seems disappointing, difficult, or boring. Go out into the world—in whatever work you find yourself—knowing that you have the chance to show people around you the kingdom of God, simply by doing your work well.

PRACTICE PERSEVERANCE: What is one way you can do your work well today and embrace the season you are currently in?

DAY 33

Live at Peace with Everyone

*"If it is possible, as far as it depends on
you, live at peace with everyone."*

ROMANS 12:18 (HCSB)

J like it when people like me. When I am in situations where I have to confront someone or clear up a misunderstanding, it makes me very uncomfortable. Conflict is not fun for me. (I'm pretty sure it's not fun for most people). But sometimes arguments and disagreements happen. Personalities clash. People who were once friends end up at odds with each other.

The Bible tells the story (in the book of Genesis) of two brothers, Jacob and Esau. They were twins, but they couldn't have been more different. One brother tricked another, hatred spewed, and the brothers stayed out of each other's lives for twenty years. During that time, however, God worked on both of their hearts, and after twenty years, they were reunited (see Genesis 33).

Relationships are hard. Sometimes relationships—whether family, friends, or co-workers—don't go the way we would like. Feelings get hurt, words are said, and cold silence reigns. It can be disappointing when friendships or relationships go through rough patches. Sometimes they are eventually restored, and sometimes both parties go opposite ways.

When I find myself in relational rough patches, I take guidance from today's verse. I can only control myself and my own actions. So I want to do whatever is possible within my power to live at peace with everyone. This may mean asking forgiveness. It may mean calling someone to talk things out. Or writing a note. How these efforts are received is completely beyond my control. I can't make the other person do anything. But I can do all within my power to make a choice for peace.

How about you, my friend? Is there a person in your life you need to make peace with? On this journey of relating to people, there will be discouraging days, but don't let your heart stay discouraged or disappointed. This will lead only to bitterness. And as the old saying goes, "Holding onto bitterness is like drinking poison and waiting for the other person to die." Your heart is too precious to hold onto unforgiveness. Choose to persevere; choose to let go and make peace today.

PRACTICE PERSEVERANCE: Who do you need to make peace with today? Remember, you can't change how the other person will react, but you can choose to live at peace as far as it depends on you. Ask God to help you let go of bitterness and embrace peace today.

PERSEVERING
in Hope

· ·

"Hope is the thing with feathers
that perches in the soul
and sings the tune without words
and never stops at all."

EMILY DICKINSON

DAY 34

Where You Focus

"We who have fled to [God] for refuge can have great
confidence as we hold to the hope that lies before us. This
hope is a strong and trustworthy anchor for our souls."

HEBREWS 6:18-19 (NLT)

I have affectionately named the GPS on my phone "Ally" (short for Allison).
She speaks in an Australian accent. I have a love/hate relationships with
GPS devices, but one fall during a short trip to Nashville, she had to guide
me to places multiple times a day, and we had no choice but to become friends.

I have a bad habit of thinking I know better than my GPS. Too many
times, I have thought, "That can't be right," and tried to find my own way,
only to realize that, yes, the GPS was correct and I should have listened. I'll
take an exit too early, or turn a different direction, only to find myself on a
dead-end street or in the middle of a parking lot. Also, I have a bad habit of
looking at the GPS map to see where I'm going next, even if the computer
voice just told me that I will be on this same road for thirty-six miles. I keep
glancing down to that steady blue line blinking up at me.

We can learn a lot of life lessons from following a GPS, I think. If God
has told me to go a certain way in life, I shouldn't keep asking to confirm it's
what He wants; until He tells me something different or changes my heart,
I should keep following the path He's put me on. He can be trusted. This is
the hope that anchors our souls. As the old saying goes, where you focus
is where you're headed.

Have you ever tried looking at a sign or something on the side of the road while you're driving? If you look that direction too long, you inevitably start swerving that direction. The same is true in our everyday lives. If we focus on money (or lack of it), people's approval, or where we are on the social ladder, then we can easily get derailed from the road God has us following.

As this verse in the book of Hebrews points out, we can have great confidence when we trust in God. He never changes, and this hope should anchor our souls firmly in faith. As we let God be our refuge, He is faithful to keep us on the right path. Will we choose to be faithful to Him and persevere in the hope He has given us? We can trust Him to lead us straight.

PRACTICE PERSEVERANCE: What have you been putting your focus on lately? Pray and ask God to put His confidence and hope within you as you trust in Him to be your refuge and give you His direction.

DAY 35

One Degree at a Time

"But when one turns to the Lord, the veil is removed.
Now the Lord is the Spirit, and where the Spirit of the
Lord is, there is freedom. And we all, with unveiled face,
beholding the glory of the Lord, are being transformed
into the same image from one degree of glory to another.
For this comes from the Lord, who is the Spirit."

2 CORINTHIANS 3:16-18 (ESV)

I once heard author and speaker Bob Goff tell a story about learning to fly a helicopter. As he got in the plane, the instructor showed him how to move the joystick around to maneuver the helicopter. Once they were up in the air, the instructor would tell him to move a little bit to the left or right to make corrections to the flight path. Instead of moving a little at a time, Bob would yank the driving stick to one side and then all the way to the other, trying to get the helicopter back on course. After a few times of being jerked wildly back and forth, his instructor yelled at Bob to stop. Then he told him, "Just make two degrees of correction a hundred times a minute, all within a space the size of a quarter."

Two degrees of correction, a hundred times a minute.

I think that's very similar to how God is instructing us to live life. We don't have to make 180-degree corrections to our choices every single day. Sometimes God is just asking us to make one degree of difference, go in a different direction by one or two degrees. I don't know about you, but when I think of it that way, it fills me with hope. I don't have to be perfect; I just have to turn towards God's voice and walk that direction. Isaiah 30:21 says, "And your ears shall hear a word behind you, saying, 'This is the way, walk in it,' when you turn to the right or when you turn to the left."

We are being transformed every day, one or two degrees at a time, closer and closer to the image and heart and character of God. It just takes time—one degree at a time. But we are changing, because we are choosing to "behold the glory of the Lord" (2 Corinthians 3:18). And what we focus on, we become.

The HCSB translation says, "We all...are looking as in a mirror at the glory of the Lord and are being transformed into the same image..."

One or two degrees at a time.

Keep focusing on God, keep persevering, keep making the small corrections He's asking you to make. Then you will become more like Him, and your life will land where He wants you. Just trust Him and listen to Him; He is the perfect navigator.

PRACTICE PERSEVERANCE: Is God asking you to make a change of one or two degrees in your life? What is that change that you can start making today?

DAY 36

God's Perspective

"For he raised us from the dead along with Christ and
seated us with Him in the heavenly realms because we
are united with Christ Jesus. So God can point to us in
all future ages as examples of the incredible wealth of
His grace and kindness toward us, as shown in all He
has done for us who are united with Christ Jesus."

EPHESIANS 2:5-7 (NLT)

When I was younger, I loved to make crafts and try to sell them. However, my marketing skills were severely lacking. Did you have the loop potholder makers when you were little? The ones with the cloth loops that you wove together? I would make dozens of these—plus a few hand-stitched pillow cases or cloth bags—sit on a picnic blanket in the front yard with my sisters, and wait for the customers to come by. If one pitying neighbor bought a potholder for a quarter, I was over the moon. I've since learned that you can't expect your customers to come to you; you need to go where they are.

Now, many years later, I am a licensed professional counselor growing a fledgling counseling practice, and an owner of a home bakery. I have come quite a ways from those days of front yard picnic blankets. But my journey has been nothing like I thought it would be. In fact, during those early days, the thought never crossed my mind that I might become an entrepreneur.

When we accept God's invitation to join His family, He enables us to see things from His perspective. We are "seated with Christ" because of what Jesus did for us. "'For My thoughts are not your thoughts, neither are your ways My ways,' declares the Lord. 'For as the heavens are higher than the earth, so are My ways higher than your ways and My thoughts than your thoughts'" (Isaiah 55:7–9, ESV). God sees things from a different perspective than we do. And I bet when He points back to us in the future generations (as Ephesians says), the path of His grace and His kindness may look different than we ever thought it would. He sees things from a higher perspective. He sees the whole journey. And even though He only chooses to show us the next step on the path, we can trust that His ways are always good.

You can hold on to hope today, my friend, because God sees the whole path. And He has given us His perspective. Sometimes there is a gap between the time God puts something on our hearts and when it comes to pass. When I was a naive kid sitting on a picnic blanket, I had no idea what God had planned for me when it came to running a business. The years passed, and I didn't even learn about business in college. But then ten years later, God planted circumstances in my path to guide me that direction.

So don't get frustrated with the gap of time between God speaking something and it actually happening. Hold onto the hope that He *did* speak to you, and be willing to hold that dream loosely; let God do with it as He sees fit. He is always faithful. He will do what He has said He will do.

PRACTICE PERSEVERANCE: Do you have an area in your life right now where you need God's wisdom to see the next step? Ask Him to give you His perspective and direction.

DAY 37

Who is My Shelter?

"For He will hide me in His shelter in the day of trouble; He will conceal me under the cover of His tent; He will lift me high upon a rock."

PSALM 27:5 (ESV)

*D*id you ever build blanket forts as a kid? When my sisters and I were little, this was one of our favorite things to do. We could be seen dragging blankets, books, chairs, and even hat racks from around the house into the room our fort was going to be. Then we would set to work building. We would spend hours in our tent playing or reading.

Last summer was my first time joining our local farmer's market. I had decided I was going to sell baked goods. When my pop-up tent was delivered (because who wants to be under the blazing Texas sun in the middle of the day?), the tent frame was missing a screw. When I'd set it up in my backyard earlier that week, it had been fine.

On the first day of farmer's market, no one showed up. It turned out their vegetables weren't ready yet, but I missed the memo that market had been cancelled. After coming with all my supplies and several dozen jumbo muffins, I decided to go ahead and set up my tent. But out on the parking lot with nothing to block the wind, the broken side of my tent was soon caving in against the wind. Try as I might to keep it stable, the tent kept collapsing, and inevitably, with a stranger stopping to help me, I had to fold it up and go back home.

I was so frustrated with this turn of events, but soon after, I read this verse in Psalm 27: "For He will hide me in His shelter...He will conceal me under the cover of His tent." I wanted my circumstances to be my shelter: everything going as planned, making a good sale, and proving to myself that I could do it. But on that day out in the parking lot, my plans failed me.

When this verse says God will shelter and cover us, He is not like my broken tent. He won't collapse on me. He never fails. He is my strong fortress. He is my rock. He is my covering and my protection.

So what have you put your hope in that has failed you? What things have been your shelter but have now collapsed? That day out in the parking lot, I learned that the money I make is not my shelter. People's approval of me is not my shelter. What is it for you? Your marriage? Friends? Your kids? Your job?

What would it look like for you to let God be your shelter? How will you choose to persevere through difficulty and let Him be your constant hope? Come under His covering, because He will not fail you. God always comes when we ask Him. He is strong and can be trusted.

PRACTICE PERSEVERANCE: Pray this prayer, "God, I see now that I have made _____ [you fill in the blank] my shelter. But it keeps falling in on me. I realize now that I have been trusting in the wrong things. Only You can be my shelter that never fails. Today I choose to hide myself in the shelter of Your rock. Will You please come and cover me in the shadow of Your wings? Thank You that You are always faithful and You never fail."

DAY 38

Hope Does Not Disappoint

"We can rejoice, too, when we run into problems and trials, for we know that they help us develop endurance. And endurance develops strength of character, and character strengthens our confident hope of salvation. And this hope will not lead to disappointment. For we know how dearly God loves us, because He has given us the Holy Spirit to fill our hearts with His love."

ROMANS 5:3-5 (NLT)

Is it possible to choose to continue living, even when this life seems dark and hopeless? Singer and songwriter Lacey Sturm is proof that, yes, you can—but not without Jesus. As a teenager, Lacey decided she was going to end her life. On the night she planned to kill herself, her grandmother sent her to church, and she had an encounter with God. She tells the story of a man whom she had never met before being brought to tears as he told her: "God doesn't want you to die tonight."

Lacey now shares her testimony and the truth of the gospel at every one of her rock concerts, including in some of the darkest places throughout the United States. She encounters people who are without hope, searching, wandering—and she shouts out the good news of Jesus to them. In an interview with Focus on the Family, she spoke these words: "It's brave to keep living." [9]

Now I have this as a reminder hanging on my office wall: To Live is Brave. To choose living—even in the midst of pain and tears—is brave.

Author Emily P. Freeman writes, "If we continue to live as though our hearts are desperately wicked, we have tragically misunderstood the work of Christ." [10]

God is not afraid of what turmoil may be inside of you. He paid the price of death so that you could have full life. He sees you, and He wants to reach in and meet you there—to touch and heal you.

But you have to let him. You have to invite him to come to your pain. He wants to heal you. Will you let Him?

If you've never let God come in and heal the pain in your life, you can pray something like this: "God, You see the hurt and brokenness in my heart. Will You come and heal me? I believe that You paid all that I owed when You died for me. And then You rose to life again and defeated death so that I can live. I believe You, and I choose to receive the life You want to give me."

PRACTICE PERSEVERANCE: If you prayed this prayer, please let me know! I'd love to be praying for you, and to connect you with some helpful resources for walking out your new journey with God! My contact information is in the back of this book.

[9] Lacey Sturm (2016). Interview by Jim Daly and John Fuller [Digital Audio Download]. Focus on the Family: How God Saved Me From Suicide (Part 1 of 2). Found at: http://www.focusonthefamily.com/media/daily-broadcast/how-god-saved-me-from-suicide-pt1

[10] Emily P. Freeman, *A Million Little Ways* (Revell, 2013), p. 52.

DAY 39

Beauty for Ashes

"To all who mourn in Israel He will give: beauty for ashes; joy
instead of mourning; praise instead of heaviness. For God has
planted them like strong and graceful oaks for His own glory."

ISAIAH 61:3 (TLB)

J love the HGTV show *Fixer Upper*. It is so inspiring that something beautiful is literally created out of the ashes—er, sawdust. The first impression of a really run-down house on the show reminds me of how we often see ourselves. Just picture it: The soon-to-be home buyers drive up and get their first look at the house.

"Oh..."

"Ugh."

"That wasn't what I was expecting."

How many times do we say the same things about ourselves? When we look at ourselves, so often we see all that is wrong and falling apart. The French artist Edgar Degas once said, "Art is not what you see, but what you make others see."[11]

God sees something different. He sees all the possibilities of who we can be. He wants to come and bring healing and beauty out of our "ashes." He has a magnificent plan to transform our lives into something amazingly beautiful.

We get the choice: Do we decide to let Him create these things in us? Do we choose to say yes to what He is designing in our lives? Because it really is up to us. What dreams has God put in your heart? What desires are stirring up in your soul? Those are from God. That is part of God's designing process.

Sometimes things don't come out in the way we think they should, or happen quite as quickly as we'd like. But God is constantly in the restoration business—and He wants to restore in you today the places that have been broken. The next verse says: "They will rebuild the ancient ruins, repairing cities destroyed long ago. They will revive them, though they have been deserted for many generations" (Isaiah 61:4 NLT).

We don't have to fix ourselves up before coming to God. We just have to ask. Will you be brave and ask today? Will you allow yourself to be made whole again by the Master Designer?

PRACTICE PERSEVERANCE: What is God restoring in your life today? Will you choose to persevere in hope by surrendering to Him? Pray and ask God for the courage to surrender to what He is building in your life, even if it looks messy at the moment.

[11] Quote from *GraceLaced* by Ruth Chou Simons (Harvest House Publishers, 2017), p. 94.

PERSEVERING
in Cultivating Gratefulness

. . . .

"Thanksgiving–giving thanks in everything–is
what prepares the way for salvation's
whole restoration."

ANN VOSKAMP, *ONE THOUSAND GIFTS*

DAY 40

Three Things a Day

"The Lord always keeps His promises; He is gracious in all He does. The Lord helps the fallen and lifts those bent beneath their loads. The eyes of all look to You in hope; You give them their food as they need it. When You open Your hand, You satisfy the hunger and thirst of every living thing. The Lord is righteous in everything He does; He is filled with kindness."

PSALM 145:13-17 (NLT)

J usually tend to default toward the negative. It's easy for me to think about the "what ifs" or dwell on what I don't have. One day several years ago, a friend told me about the book One Thousand Gifts by Ann Voskamp. In this book, she outlines a practice she started of writing down three things each day she was thankful for. If you write just three things every day, by the end of a year, you have counted over one thousand gifts God has given you. They don't have to be big things; in fact, some of the ones I've written down over the years may seem downright insignificant. For about two years, I wrote in a gratitude journal every day. And I can say that this practice changed my life.

While I no longer write things down (except occasionally in my journal), I am able to quickly redirect myself when I start looking at the negative. I take a deep breath and choose to think differently. I will even say it out loud if possible: "Right now, I am thankful for...." And my heart immediately changes. My anxiety levels go down. And I'm able to see my world completely differently within a few seconds.

So look around you right now. What can you find to be thankful for? It doesn't have to be complicated; most gifts are simple.

- Soapy bubbles in the sink
- Kids' toys all over the floor—evidence of fun playing together
- Bare feet
- A soft blanket and good-smelling lotion
- Good hugs
- Encouraging words from a friend

You might be surprised at the gifts you can find if you open your eyes to look for them.

PRACTICE PERSEVERANCE: List three things each day this week to be thankful for. You can use a notebook, the notes section of your phone, take pictures to post on Instagram, or write in the blank space of this page. (If you share on social media, add the tag #sacredtenacity; I'd love to see your gratitude lists!) Ask God to open your eyes to His gifts around you each day and to develop in you a heart of gratitude.

DAY 41

Champion Each Other

> "Just as our bodies have many parts and each part has a
> special function, so it is with Christ's body. We are many
> parts of one body, and we all belong to each other."
>
> ROMANS 12:4-5 (NLT)

*H*ave you ever broken your arm? What about your nose, thumb, or pinky toe? Those last few examples may seem small compared to having a whole arm out of commission, but have you ever tried walking on a foot that has a fractured pinky toe?

The apostle Paul, who was writing to the church in Rome, compares us as believers to a human body. There are so many parts, big and small, but each of us have a role to play in order for the whole body to function.

When I was in middle school, my church hosted a youth weekend retreat. At the home where the girls were assigned, most of the girls spread out their sleeping bags in the living room and made pallets on the floor. There was not room for all of us to fit in the living room, so my twin sister and I moved to an adjoining room and laid down to sleep.

True to the nature of junior high and high school students, the girls in the living room stayed up talking long after lights out. However, as I lay in my sleeping bag that night, I heard the topic of conversation change from the light-hearted topics of music and nail polish colors. One of the older girls was speaking quite loudly; I could hear everything she said. She was talking about me and my sister, as if we weren't just in the next room. She scoffed at how quiet we were (compared to the others) and ridiculed the fact we were homeschooled. The word "weird" was thrown around quite a few times. I was shocked to hear others agree with her. And the main attitude that struck me and sat heavily on my chest as I lay there listening was that she very much thought I didn't fit in and I definitely didn't belong with "them."

We live in a culture today that often pits women against men, and even women against other women. This is seen even within the Church! Since my writing is primarily to women, I'm going to address you for a moment. The apostle Paul writes, "If you bite and devour one another, watch out that you are not consumed by one another" (Galatians 5:15, ESV). He's talking to Christians here. We have the power within us to destroy each other if we are not careful. We have an enemy who is wanting to destroy our unity as the Church. In order to win, we have to fight together—not fight each other.

It's been said that life is simple until people get involved. Loving others can be difficult, especially when they are very different than us. With women especially, comparison is so rampant. We get jealous of what someone else has, and so we talk badly about them. We see the happy, smiling pictures on social media and despair that our lives are not so perfect. Instead of rejoicing with each other, we pull each other down with our words and our actions. This should not be! We as women should be celebrating with the joys of other women. We'd want them to do the same for us, right? There is power in women encouraging and empowering one another. Celebrating our sisters in Christ is so counter-cultural, and that's why it's so powerful.

And let's not forget the men around us. Listen to me here: Godly men are a gift to us as women. Men and women offer strength in different ways. I am so thankful for the brothers and fathers and pastors and leaders in my life. I never had older brothers growing up, but now, because of the men in my church, I have several "brothers" (younger and older) whom I get to live life with. I have been able to serve alongside them, and they have encouraged me with their words and actions. They have challenged me and prayed for me. And they have taught me to be strong in who I am.

The worldly culture tells us that we need to look out for ourselves, and only if we push and claw our way to the top will we be successful. But we are not meant to travel this journey alone. Celebrating, encouraging, and helping others along the way does not rob us of strength. It makes us stronger. "Though one may be overpowered, two can defend themselves. A cord of three strands is not quickly broken" (Ecclesiastes 4:12, NIV).

Let's continue to persevere by learning to cultivate gratitude toward one another. Your strength is needed. My strength is needed. There is room for each of us. What would happen if we chose to link arms with the men and women around us, be grateful for them and what they bring to the table, and walk together in the things God has for us? What would happen if we learned to be grateful for each other? Each person God has put around you is a gift.

PRACTICE PERSEVERANCE: Thank God for the gifts of the other women and men around you. Write a quick text or hand-written note thanking a specific person today for the strengths and gifts they offer you through who they are.

DAY 42

A Mindset Shift

"And God will generously provide all you need.
Then you will always have everything you need
and plenty left over to share with others."

2 CORINTHIANS 9:8 (NLT)

I've spent the majority of the time writing this book while trying to grow two small businesses. I recently made the shift to grow my counseling practice by committing more time to it (a.k.a. quitting my day job) while at the same time working on the startup of a home bakery. I'm doing two things that I love, and it makes me happy. But it is a LOT of really hard work. And there have been times when things were tight financially. It is a test of faith to start a small or side business. Every day I have a choice: Will I be worried and anxious about making ends meet, or will I choose to do my best, be grateful, and enjoy the journey?

During the summer, I get the opportunity to sell my baked goods at a local farmer's market. Some days are good, and some days are not. It's hard not to get discouraged on the bad days. But I've learned a valuable lesson during this time: Provision is not the same as money. I ask—and believe—that God will provide for me. But sometimes that's not tied to a specific amount of money. Sometimes it's the fact that I got to trade homemade muffins for fresh yellow squash and zucchini at the farmer's market. That is provision. I am learning to see these opportunities as answers to my prayers and choosing to be grateful.

We can't be grateful and anxious at the same time.

As we choose to intentionally be grateful, even in the smallest of things, we start to see God's blessings and provisions everywhere.

- Fresh veggies from a friend's garden.
- Farm fresh eggs.

- Time spent with family or friends.
- A worship song coming on the radio at just the right moment.
- An encouraging word.
- Library books.
- Fresh flowers (even wildflowers).
- Rain showers.
- Friends who are neighbors and neighbors who are friends.

Perseverance is required when learning to daily practice gratefulness. In cultivating gratitude, our hearts begin to change. And instead of our default mode being anxiety and fearing the worst, we begin to see how loving our God is, and how much He really has given us.

PRACTICE PERSEVERANCE: Take a piece of paper, open the notes section of your phone, or use the blank space on this page and list three ways that God has provided for you this week. Take time to thank God right now for always generously providing all you need.

DAY 43

Receive His Blessings

"All praise to God, the Father of our Lord Jesus Christ, who has
blessed us with every spiritual blessing in the heavenly realms
because we are united with Christ. Even before He made the world,
God loved us and chose us in Christ to be holy and without fault in
His eyes. God decided in advance to adopt us into His own family
by bringing us to Himself through Jesus Christ. This is what He
wanted to do, and it gave Him great pleasure...He has showered
His kindness on us, along with all wisdom and understanding."

EPHESIANS 1:3-5,8 (NLT)

O n an unusually warm day for January, I was out walking in my neighborhood, enjoying the fresh air. As I was walking, just down the street
in front of me there was a UPS truck delivering packages. As the UPS
man got out of the truck, he jogged up to each house with his hands full
of boxes, and then jogged back to his truck. He drove down a few houses
farther and did it again. He ran up to the house and ran back. I watched him
do this over and over again.

Now, I don't know if he had a deadline he had to make, or he just wanted to
get home sooner for dinner. But watching this man got me thinking: Is this how
God is with us? He's running towards us, His hands full of blessings. He can't
wait to give us what He's wrapped up just for us. And it's going to be good!

Today's verse says God chose to *adopt* us into His family, and this gave
Him great pleasure. He has made each of us a part of His family; all we have
to do is to say yes. It's better than Christmas! Unlike gifts under a tree that
may get set aside sooner or later, God's gifts never wear out and never go
out of style. His gifts to us last forever, and they can never be taken away.

So many times, I think we forget to keep our eyes open for God's beautiful blessings every day. We get so caught up in our own busy lives, or we get

overwhelmed with all that seems to be going wrong around us. I know I do. But what if we chose to receive God's blessings today? What if we chose to persevere in cultivating hearts of gratitude? What if we chose to believe His Word that says He has *good* plans for us, not plans to harm us? He delights in giving good gifts to His children.

He's running at us, His arms full of blessings. Choose to receive God's gifts today, my friend. You will be glad you did.

PRACTICE PERSEVERANCE: What is one blessing God has given you today that you can choose to be thankful for? Take a few minutes to thank God for this blessing right now, either out loud or by writing it here.

DAY 44

When the Answer Is Different

"See that no one pays back evil for evil, but always try to
do good to each other and to all people. Always be joyful.
Never stop praying. Be thankful in all circumstances, for
this is God's will for you who belong to Christ Jesus."

1 THESSALONIANS 5:15-18 (NLT)

*J*n one of my favorite books, *The Hiding Place*, author and speaker
Corrie ten Boom tells her family's story of helping to hid Jews in their
Amsterdam home during World War II, and their subsequent imprison-
ment in the German concentration camps. When Corrie and her sister Betsie
entered their quarters at the women's camp of Ravensbruck, they quickly
discovered the over-crowded sleeping cots were riddled with fleas. As
Corrie despaired, Betsie remembered the verse they had read that morning
from their tiny Bible that had miraculously escaped inspection. "Give thanks
in all circumstances..."

"That's what we can do. We can start right now to thank God for
every single thing about this new barracks!"
I stared at her, then around me at the dark, foul-aired room.
"Such as?" I said.
"Such as being assigned here together."
I bit my lip. "Oh yes, Lord Jesus!"
"Such as what you're holding in your hands."
I looked down at the Bible. "Yes! Thank You, dear Lord, that there

was no inspection when we entered here! Thank You for all the women, here in this room, who will meet You in these pages."

"Yes," said Betsie. "Thank You for the very crowding here. Since we're packed so close, that many more will hear!" She looked at me expectantly. "Corrie!" she prodded.

"Oh, all right. Thank You for the jammed, crammed, stuffed, packed, suffocating crowds."

"Thank You," Betsie went on serenely, "for the fleas and for—"

The fleas! This was too much. "Betsie, there's no way even God can make me grateful for a flea."

"'Give thanks in *all* circumstances,'" she quoted. "It doesn't say, 'in pleasant circumstances.' Fleas are part of this place where God has put us."

And so we stood between piers of bunks and gave thanks for fleas.[12]

It turned out that the ladies had more time in this building to read from their little Bible, pray, and worship out loud with the other women who were taken from countries all over Europe. Later, Betsie overheard an argument between the guards, because every one of them refused to cross the threshold into this barracks. The reason? The place was swarming with fleas!

So the fleas did end up being an upside-down kind of blessing from God. And sometimes His provision to us may look "upside-down," too. It may not look anything like what we'd prayed for. But it brings blessings nonetheless.

Maybe you have a child with special needs, and raising him or her is very difficult. But at the same time, you've learned through experiences with your little one about the kindness and joy of God. Maybe you or someone close to you struggles with a chronic illness or disability, but you've learned through these experiences to lean into God's strength when you feel at your weakest.

We may not see the reason for our pain and trials this side of heaven. We probably will never get answers to our "why." But we can choose to persevere and trust that God sees us, He sees the big picture, and He knows our pain. He will not leave us alone, and He will continue to give us what we need, even if it looks different than we thought.

PRACTICE PERSEVERANCE: Do you find yourself in a situation today where it's hard to be thankful? Ask God to show you things to be thankful for, even when they may seem to be "upside down" gifts. Ask God for what you need, and keep your eyes open for the answer, even if it looks different than you thought.

[12] Corrie ten Boom, *The Hiding Place* (Chosen Books, 1971), p. 180–181.

PERSEVERING
in Encouraging Others

....

"And there is freedom in knowing that God made us just
the way we are for a reason. That maybe the thing we
do well is exactly what our friend or loved one needs...
The beauty in showing up, in choosing to enter the dance
even though you might not know the steps, is that God
creates something beautiful from our attempts."

KARA TIPPETTS AND JILL LYNN BUTEYN,
JUST SHOW UP

DAY 45

How Are You Gifted?

"Yes, the body has many different parts, not just one part. If the foot says, "I am not a part of the body because I am not a hand," that does not make it any less a part of the body. And if the ear says, "I am not part of the body because I am not an eye," would that make it any less a part of the body? If the whole body were an eye, how would you hear? Or if your whole body were an ear, how would you smell anything? But our bodies have many parts, and God has put each part just where He wants it."

1 CORINTHIANS 12:14-18 (NLT)

After one of my major surgeries, I was staying with my parents during the summer for recovery. One afternoon my parents decided to run some errands. My sister was there, and I said I'd be fine. Not even ten minutes after they were gone, something went wrong with my wound care machine and I had to call the home health nurse to come out and fix it. I was so frustrated with how helpless I felt that I burst into tears. I plopped down on my bed with my sister looking on. "I hate this!" I sobbed. "Is this how it's always going to be?! If it's always going to be this way, I don't want to do this anymore!"

Just then my cell phone rang. As I made my way to the phone, I told my sister that if it wasn't my parents or Mark or Kathy from my church, I wasn't going to answer. It was Mark. I took a deep breath and picked up the phone. "Hello?"

Mark immediately knew something was up. "You sound out of breath," he said.

"I've been crying," I admitted. I didn't have to tell him much, and he quickly asked if he could pray for me. He started praying out loud with me on the phone. During this season of my life, I felt very far from God. Not that I didn't believe He was with me, but I couldn't feel Him with me like I usually could, and this had never happened before. I felt like I was existing in a bubble. As Mark prayed over me that day, I remember him praying that God's presence would be with me strongly. He said God gave him a picture of His presence filling up my bedroom. More tears came. God knew what I needed. God saw me in this moment and came for me.

What I didn't find out until years later was that Mark was thinking about me and had decided to call me sometime soon. However, at that moment, he felt God tell him, "No, call her right now." He had no idea what that simple act of obedience meant to me, or how it would encourage my heart. He told me later, "I was just doing what I would normally do." For him, picking up the phone and calling someone was easy. But it changed my whole day.

You don't have to encourage someone the same way Mark did. It might look different for you. How are you gifted? What comes naturally to you? Use that to reach out to people. Even a quick text message or email could mean the world to someone. People just want to know they are being seen and thought of. If you have someone who's been on your heart and mind, chances are God is the one who put him or her there. We are naturally selfish and think of ourselves the most (and first). If we are thinking of someone else, that is evidence that God wants us to pray for them and reach out to them.

It can be as simple as, "I'm thinking about you today. Anything I can pray for you?" Of course, handwritten cards and personal phone calls are also great connectors. When someone comes to mind, don't brush it off. Be intentional to take a few minutes and connect with them. It may seem uncomfortable at first, but persevere through the awkward moments. You never know what kind of an impact your one simple act of obedience might have.

PRACTICE PERSEVERANCE: In what ways are you gifted to encourage people? How can you plan to be intentional in using this gift to connect with those around you?

DAY 46

Following Up

"Love one another with brotherly affection.
Outdo one another in showing honor."

ROMANS 12:10 (ESV)

*D*uring and shortly after college, I was on the leadership team of my church's college ministry. There were about ten of us, and we were the ones who pitched in to bring food or snacks each week, prayed together before group started, greeted at the door, and cleaned up after group. My friend and one of my mentors, Kathy, led the group with her husband Mark. Kathy has taught me over the years the importance of following up with people. When someone in small group shares something going on in their life, or someone asks me to pray for them, it is important to follow up with them a few days later. This is part of loving them and showing them honor.

When I worked with the college group, Kathy would often ask us to follow up with specific people who might be new or struggling with a specific problem. This taught me to be intentional. Usually it was a phone call, but sometimes it was a text to see how they were doing. (When you work with college students, or anybody for that matter, connect in the way that reaches them best.) Later, when I started opening my home for an adult small group, I would often be given names of people new to the church who I would invite to get connected with our small group.

People want to know that they are seen and feel that they belong. Following up and making sure people feel heard and get connected is simple, but it must be intentional. This is part of being connected to the body of Christ. It's not normal for our human nature to be thinking of other people. But if we are to die to ourselves as Jesus told us, we have to quit thinking of ourselves all the time.

Reaching out to others takes perseverance, because sometimes people don't act like they want connection. When I text or call someone, sometimes I get a response back, and sometimes I don't. But even if the person doesn't reply back, don't take it personally. You know you were obedient, and at least the person knows in that moment they are being thought of and they are cared for.

PRACTICE PERSEVERANCE: Who is one person on your heart that you can reach out to and encourage? What is one specific way you can follow up and connect with that person this week?

DAY 47

Put It on the Calendar

"Where there is no revelation, people cast off restraint;
but blessed is the one who heeds wisdom's instruction."

PROVERBS 29:18 (NIV)

*D*o you use a printed calendar or planner? Or is your calendar on your phone? I used to carry two small planners in my purse: one for work and one for personal. Finally a friend told me I could put them both on my phone calendar. "But then I'll get my schedules mixed up!" I protested. She informed me that I could color-code them. Now, I don't just have two colors for personal and work schedules. If you were to look at my phone calendar, I have about five or six colors going on for various things. It looks crazy, but it helps me stay sane.

I've also learned that unless something gets put on my calendar, it will most likely not get done. This includes time with friends. Yes, I literally schedule times to visit or even call friends into my calendar. This may sound impersonal, but unless I have that reminder ding and tell me to give someone a call, I will get so caught up in my busy day and constantly tell myself, "I need to call her sometime." But sometime never comes.

You may find a different system that works for you. But if we are going to choose to be intentional in connecting as the body of Christ, maintaining healthy relationships, and making people feel seen and heard, we have to make a plan. Habakkuk 2:2 says, "Write the vision; make it plain on tablets, so he may run who reads it" (ESV). Once the vision was written down, a runner would run and take it to the surrounding people, so that everyone knew what God was telling them. If we don't make a plan and write down how we are going to live this life, then chances are we will end up in a place we didn't expect to be.

Just as personal and business goals need to be written down so we can see where we're headed, relational goals need to be made clear, too. This includes strengthening existing relationships and building new ones. I have a list on my phone of friends I want to have lunch or coffee with, and I try to meet with one of these friends at least once or twice a month. But we have to be intentional and schedule it. I also have grandparents and a friend who live out of state that I either call or FaceTime on a regular basis. But you can bet it's put in my calendar ahead of time. Maybe you're not as much of a list person as I am. (In fact, you're probably not.) But it's still so important to be intentional about how we plan our time. What is on your calendar shows what (and who) is most important to you.

God does His work in this world primarily through His people. And people are important to Him. We never know what someone's going through. Everyone has a story. And everyone's story matters dearly to God. Will we choose to be a part of showing people they are valuable? Will we choose to persevere and make time to show them they are important and loved?

PRACTICE PERSEVERANCE: Pull out your calendar and start making a plan for your relationships. How can you block out time to invest in your existing relationships? How can you make time to build new ones and let people know they belong?

DAY 48

Keep Showing Up

"The Israelites out-fought the Amalekites as long as Moses
held up his arms, but they started losing whenever he had
to lower them. Finally, Moses was so tired that Aaron and
Hur got a rock for him to sit on. Then they stood beside him
and supported his arms in the same position until sunset."

EXODUS 17:11–12 (CEV)

J have friends who hardly ever answer text messages. (You know who you are!) At first, this really bothered me. But when I talked with them about it, they said they got busy and never went back to answer their phone messages. I learned not to take it personally. With other friends, if I'm asking them a question and I don't get a response back, I know the answer is "no." Time has taught me this. So I learned not to take that personally, either. But then I have other friends: if they don't text back within a day or so, something might be wrong.

One thing I've learned about following through with people who are hurting: don't give up. Keep showing up. Keep texting or calling them (although don't turn into a stalker). Keep asking them how they're doing. And then be okay if they don't know how they're doing. Getting an answer is not the point. Showing hurting friends that they are important and cared for and loved is the point.

When I was 21 years old, I had emergency surgery and was in the hospital for almost a month, with multiple surgeries following. During that time, people brought food to my family, showered me with cards, and covered me in prayer. I still remember the first meal I had the day I came home with my family from the hospital. It was enchiladas and soup from a neighbor, which my mom had been able to put in the freezer a couple of weeks before.

When life gets hard, don't back down. Press in. We've all been touched in one way or another by some of life's greatest tragedies:

- Cancer
- Alzheimer's
- Lost pregnancy
- Lost job
- Hospitalization
- Failed adoption
- The list goes on...

What happens when it's someone you love?

One of the best practical resources I've found in the area of reaching out to those who are struggling is the book *The Art of Helping* by Lauren Littauer Briggs. It is more than just another book; It helps us see the heart behind reaching out to others, and it has lots of very practical ideas for a variety of situations (moving, new baby, grief and loss, hospital and surgery, parenting challenges).

I had one friend during my recovery months who always took the time to listen to me. And she always asked the questions everyone else was afraid to ask. Instead of offending me, this really meant a lot to me. I appreciated that someone really took the time to ask what was going on and how I felt about it (even when I didn't know or just cried instead).

We are meant to live life in community with other people. We need each other—especially when life gets hard. Keep persevering by showing up in the difficult places. Don't be afraid to ask questions. And don't be afraid if there are no answers. Be brave and show up anyway. This world needs you.

PRACTICE PERSEVERANCE: Who is one person you can reach out to today who is going through something difficult? Give them a call, bring them a gift, or do something else to encourage them today.

DAY 49

Speak the Truth in Love

"Instead, we will speak the truth in love, growing in every way more and more like Christ, who is the head of His body, the church. He makes the whole body fit together perfectly. As each part does its own special work, it helps the other parts grow, so that the whole body is healthy and growing and full of love."

EPHESIANS 4:15–16 (NLT)

*D*o you remember having "growing pains" when you were younger? Random parts of your body would ache and hurt, because literally bones and muscles and tendons were growing to make you taller and stronger. Sometimes I would start crying because my legs would hurt and ache so bad, and my mom would come in and massage them. "It's okay," she would say. "It means you're growing."

Just like a human body, the Church body is meant to be healthy and growing. One of the ways we do that is to speak the truth to each other in love. This can be a painful part of the growing process, but just like growing pains when you were younger, it is a necessary part of the growing process as a Church body.

My friend Julie (who I mentioned briefly on Day 8) is so gifted at speaking the truth in love. And I really do mean it is a gift. She is willing to tell things to you straight, but she does it in a way that is gentle. You know she truly cares for you as a person, even if what she said may sting a little. This is a gift for us. If you have a friend like this, don't turn away from them. Such people are often able to see things we may not, and they help us get back on the path God has for us.

Speaking the truth means saying what God says in His Word, and reflecting His heart to others around us in what we say. Speaking the truth *in love* means as we lead people to God's truth, we always keep in mind that they are made in the image of God and are fully loved by Him. The truth hurts sometimes, but truth spoken in love is always meant to *heal* in the end.

Paul says in this verse that when we speak the truth to each other in love, it makes us as a Church grow to be full and healthy. This will take perseverance on our part because giving and receiving truth is not always easy. Do you want to grow? Then you will need to receive the loving truth godly people speak into your life.

PRACTICE PERSEVERANCE: Who in your life has permission to speak God's truth in love to you? Who do you need to speak truth to in love?

DAY 50

Words Change the Course of Life

"The tongue has the power of life and death,
and those who love it will eat its fruit."

PROVERBS 18:21 (NIV)

Over the years, I have had so many people speak words of life over me. Of course, I have also had people speak words that brought death. But as I focus on the life-giving words, the words of death begin to lose their power. As I look back over previous journals, I am so grateful that people in my life took the time to speak to me about who I am and the plans God has for my life. Words can literally change the course of a person's life—for better or for worse.

I'm kind of a slow learner when it comes to believing the truth about who I am. I often have to hear the same truth several times before I actually believe it. But I'm getting better at believing the truth faster now. I remember one specific time that my friend Brad spoke life over me. He told me one day, "God has plans for your life. Do not be afraid." This was not the first time he had spoken encouraging words to me. But on this day, something inside me shifted. It was like a light switch got turned on. As I was thinking about his words, I made a conscious decision: I was not going to just wish this was true. I was not going to think it was true for somebody else but not for me. No, I was going to fiercely grab hold of this truth and believe that it was true for me. After that, I began to be more confident and actually believe what

God said. That moment was a turning point for me to start living out of who God says I am instead of living out of fear.

I am fortunate to have had many, many people choose to see the best in me and encourage me in who God has created me to be. Sometimes they've had to correct me along the way, because I can make poor choices occasionally. But mostly, they choose to speak life (in spite of my humanity) because they see what God has put in me.

What about you? Do you have people who can speak encouragement and life and godly instruction to you? Do you have people who can tell you out loud who they see God is creating you to be? If not, ask God to open your eyes to who around you can be these kinds of people. What about the words you speak to others? Are they words of life or words of death? Are you encouraging and building others up, or tearing them down?

You may never know what your words mean to those you speak to, or how they will react to them. But only you can decide what to do with the words spoken to you. It is your choice to receive words of truth or not. And hearing life-giving words is not enough. It is only in believing and acting on God's truth spoken to you that you can continue to grow.

PRACTICE PERSEVERANCE: Ask God to empower you to speak life to the people around you this week. Ask Him to show you what He sees in people, and choose to speak those things out loud to them. Ask God to give you His ability to believe the truth when others speak life to you, too.

PERSEVERING
in Serving

"All we can do is take what He has given to us and offer it back to Him in the form of giving it away to others. Our offerings aren't efforts worked up inside ourselves. Our offerings are unique responses to a living, giving God."

EMILY P. FREEMAN, *A MILLION LITTLE WAYS*

DAY 51

When You Don't Feel Like It

"As soon as I pray, You answer me;
You encourage me by giving me strength."

PSALM 138:3 (NLT)

A couple of years ago, I began opening my home to host one of our church's weekly small groups. I love having people in my home, fixing good food, and creating a welcoming place. Even cleaning my house has a sense of anticipation to it when I know someone is coming over. However, I am not always happy to clean and organize and cook. Some days I just don't feel like doing it. I'm tired, and I want to be a hermit in the house all by myself.

That's when I have to let God strengthen me. He has put this opportunity to serve in front of me, and He will give me the strength to do it. God doesn't tell us not to be tired. But when we do get tired and discouraged, He wants us to come to Him for strength and encouragement. How? Well, just like today's verse says: we pray. Just speak to God and tell Him how you're feeling. It's okay, He can handle it. He's not going to think you're "less" of a Christian because you get worn out. Be honest with Him. Then ask Him to strengthen you.

Nehemiah did this when God called him to lead an incredible building project to put up a wall to protect the entire city of Jerusalem, all while Israel's enemies taunted and jeered and tried to stop the project. Nehemiah prayed,

"But now, O God, strengthen my hands" (Nehemiah 6:9, ESV). This is what it means to persevere—serving in God's strength, not our own.

Last but not least, ask someone else to pray with you and for you. We are not meant to live this life alone. Especially when it comes to serving the Church as the people of God, we are meant to have each other's backs and stand by each other with the strength that God gives us. So find someone you trust to pray for you, encourage you, and remind you that you are not alone.

This season will not always be hard. Keep fighting the battle. Keep being faithful to what God has called you to do. Keep persevering with sacred tenacity.

PRACTICE PERSEVERANCE: What is wearing you down right now? Find someone to pray for you, and together ask God to give you the strength to do what He is calling you to do for this season of your life.

DAY 52

Saying No to Isolation

"And let us consider how to stir up one another to love
and good works, not neglecting to meet together, as is
the habit of some, but encouraging one another, and
all the more as you see the Day drawing near."

HEBREWS 10:24-25 (ESV)

*I*s there something you've always grown up doing, and never ques-
tioned? And then one day, did you realize that maybe you were just
doing it because you "should"? Sometime last year, I got to the point that
I didn't want to go to church on Sunday morning. I've grown up in church,
and I have never thought twice about where I will be on Sunday mornings.
However, during this time, due to several different factors, I found myself
honestly not wanting to go.

I recognized this, and so I started talking to God about it. I told Him I just
wanted to stay home and bake cupcakes (seriously!). But I also know that—
for me—if I started giving in to that urge, it would turn into a habit. Staying
home next time would only get easier. And, slowly, I would move away from
the wise and encouraging people I need in my life.

I can tend to be such a hermit sometimes—and actually like it. There are
certainly times for that; but I need other people around me, too.

As I prayed, God brought this verse to my mind: "Whoever isolates
himself seeks his own desire; he breaks out against all sound judgment"
(Proverbs 18:1, ESV). Another translation says, "He breaks out against all
good sense."

I don't know about you, but I want to have good sense. The writer of Hebrews also notes: "But encourage one another daily, as long as it is called 'Today,' so that none of you may be hardened by sin's deceitfulness" (Hebrews 3:13, NIV). If we don't intentionally choose to surround ourselves with people who will encourage us and point us to God's Word (which means challenging us when needed), then our hearts will get hardened by the temptation of sin. Yes, in my story, this was a temptation. And yes, it would have grown into sin.

Why? Because the person who isolates themselves rebels against all sound judgement. And when I refuse to listen to the wisdom of God, that is sin.

In the end, I decided to go to church not because I felt like I "should" anymore, but because I decided to choose in this moment to say yes to God. I chose to persevere in obedience.

God has created us to live in community. Finding good, healthy, life-giving relationships takes lots of time and hard work. But don't run away because it's hard. Persevere. Press past the awkward. Be willing to step out and go. Say yes to letting people into your life.

PRACTICE PERSEVERANCE: In what ways are you tempted to isolate yourself? Ask God to show you how to develop relationships with a healthy community of people.

DAY 53

Run in Your Lane

"Therefore, since we are surrounded by such a huge crowd of witnesses to the life of faith, let us strip off every weight that slows us down, especially the sin that so easily trips us up. And let us run with endurance the race God has set before us. We do this by keeping our eyes on Jesus, the champion who initiates and perfects our faith."

HEBREWS 12:1–2 (NLT)

I started coming to my current church when I was in college. When I first joined, I was involved in almost everything. My church was a lot smaller back then, but I still said yes to so many things. If a volunteer was needed in the nursery, I said yes. If there was a new discipleship class or Bible study, I said yes. Any time someone asked if I was available, I said yes.

Pretty soon I was starting to feel burned out. I was tired. One day, I was complaining to my friend and mentor Kathy about how busy I was, and she challenged me with something. She told me, "Our pastors don't want you to say yes to everything. They would much rather you say yes to one or two things that you are good at and really enjoy." It seems simple, but that was such a relief to me. For some reason, I felt like I had to do all the things in order to prove myself. But I didn't. Kathy's words gave me permission to say yes to a few good things and "run in my lane."

What does it mean to "run in your lane"? These are the activities that most excite you. These are the opportunities that bring you a sense of purpose and get you up in the morning. These are the tasks that you feel you are really good at. What are those in your life? Say yes to those things (even if it's just one or two) and let the rest go.

This doesn't mean the things you quit doing are bad. Chances are, they are actually really good things. So why would you stop doing things in your life that are good? Oswald Chambers writes in his devotional book *My Utmost for His Highest*: "The good is always the enemy of the best...We have to learn to walk according to the standard which has its eyes focused on God." Sometimes, in order to focus on what are the "best" things in our lives *for this moment*, we have to quit doing some "good" things.

Have you ever tried to balance a yardstick with your finger? You place your hand in the middle, right? And it should balance just fine. But if you put a weight on one end (let's say a small rock), then you can no longer place your fingers in the middle. You have to move them over toward the rock in order for the yardstick to balance again.

The same is true in life: When something is weighing more heavily in one area of life, we have to move our attention more towards that thing. This means the stuff on the other end of the "yardstick" of our lives may be put on the back burner for a while—or may be ignored completely.

When most people read today's verse, they focus on "the sin that so easily trips us up." But what about the things that are not sin, but they slow us down? What keeps you from running with perseverance the race God has set before you? Do you need to quit doing some good things in order to do the things that are best? It will look different for each person. It will also change depending on your current season in life. The things you quit doing are probably not sinful things. They are probably good, helpful, holy, kingdom things. But for you at this moment, they may not the right things.

PRACTICE PERSEVERANCE: What race has God called you to run with perseverance? What things slow you down that you need to remove today (or make a plan to remove in the near future)?

DAY 54

A Pleasure to Serve

"Jesus called them together and said, 'You know that the rulers
in this world lord it over their people, and officials flaunt their
authority over those under them. But among you it will be
different. Whoever wants to be a leader among you must be your
servant, and whoever wants to be first among you must become
your slave. For even the Son of Man came not to be served but
to serve others and to give His life as a ransom for many.'"

MATTHEW 20:25–28 (NLT)

Sometimes I watch a show on Netflix called *Chef's Table*. It highlights chefs from around the world, what they create in their kitchens, and how they got to where they are. Do you know what chefs call the evenings when customers come in to sit at their tables and eat? They call it service. Literally. As in, "We're preparing our dishes for tonight's service." Think about it: Chefs spend hours and days preparing beautiful, intricate dishes for people to eat; they scour the local farms for fresh, seasonal ingredients; they are constantly coming up with new ideas and innovations—and they call it service.

What if we took that same view for all of life? Life is about service to others. It's not about how fancy we can make things. It's about serving the people around us so they feel seen and cared for.

When I was a senior in high school, I took a trip to Germany where we built relationships with local people, learned from the missionaries there about their work, and prayer-walked the nearby neighborhoods. One of the teachings we heard was about the "top line" and "bottom line" in God's kingdom. The "top line" means something important to God's heart: He wants to bless us. Throughout Scripture, we see that God is good and He desires to bless us and give us good things. However, that is not the whole picture. The "bottom line"—the most important mission in God's kingdom and heart—is that He would be given all the glory.

He is God, after all. He created all things and holds them all together. His one aim for us as humans is to get to a place that we surrender all of our agendas and pride and opinions and raise Him to His rightful place—above everything that can be named. He deserves all the glory. And the sole aim of everything He does in His kingdom, the "bottom line," is that He is given all the glory.

When we serve others, are we doing it for God's glory or for our own? Are we wanting to be recognized and praised? Or are we simply obeying God and reflecting Him in what we do?

I know I have been guilty of wanting recognition and my own glory many times. *I've worked so hard at this, can't you see what a great job I did?* But that's not how God's kingdom works. If I want to be a working, whole, and useful part of God's kingdom, I obey in response to God and as a result of wanting Him to get the praise. When I love Him, I will want to honor Him. This requires perseverance, because it means daily choosing humility.

As servants of God, this does not mean we are cogs in a wheel. Please don't misunderstand me. God is not sitting on His throne waiting to crush us if we mess up. He is a good, caring, loving King. But He is the King. And He is the one who deserves all the honor and glory and praise.

PRACTICE PERSEVERANCE: How is God calling you to serve Him by serving others today? Ask God to give you a heart to serve others for His glory, not your own.

DAY 55

Honoring Godly Leaders

"Have confidence in your leaders and submit to their
authority, because they keep watch over you as those who
must give an account. Do this so that their work will be a
joy, not a burden, for that would be of no benefit to you."

HEBREWS 13:17 (NIV)

*D*uring the week I am writing this, there was a pastor in the news who committed suicide. He had struggled with depression for many years, had been honest with his struggles, and had gotten help. From all accounts, he had been very brave in handling his struggle. But in the end, it proved too much to bear. This makes me sad, that someone would think that those around them would be better off without them, especially a pastor. But pastors are people, too. They don't have superpowers that make them immune. They struggle just like the rest of us.

That is why it is so important to pray for our pastors and church leaders. True, they are human, but they have also been given responsibility to care for and guide the people of God. Many of us have no idea what kind of a burden that can be. Even if you don't always agree with your spiritual leaders, you can pray for them. Pray that God will fill them with His wisdom and the anointing of His Holy Spirit. Pray that God will guide them and protect them and their families. Then look for practical ways to reach out. Send them an encouraging note. Tell them you are praying for them. And as long as they are following God's Word, honor their decisions, even if you think you would have chosen differently.

God has placed your pastors and church leaders in their positions for a reason. They have been called to lead and direct your church. So pray that they are guided in God's ways, because the direction they are going is the direction the whole church will end up going. Pray for perseverance—that your pastors will have God's strength and empowerment to do what God has put in front of them to do. Pray that your leaders will immerse themselves in God's Word and hear clearly from God about His people. Honor your leaders when they set healthy boundaries (like deciding to go on vacation with their families or not taking phone calls for a period of time). Pray that they will get rest and their hearts will be encouraged.

Our health and growth as a Church depends largely on the health and growth of our spiritual leaders. Why? Because, even though we are responsible for maturing and growing ourselves individually, God has placed a special calling on our pastors and other church leaders to guide us as a Church body to grow in unity together and reach out to our surrounding communities.

PRACTICE PERSEVERANCE: Take a few minutes to pray for your pastor and church leaders by name today. Pray that they will hear from God and be filled with the wisdom and knowledge that only He can give.

DAY 56

On Mission

"So prepare your minds for action and exercise self-control.
Put all your hope in the gracious salvation that will come
to you when Jesus Christ is revealed to the world. So you
must live as God's obedient children. Don't slip back into
your old ways of living to satisfy your own desires. You
didn't know any better then. But now you must be holy in
everything you do, just as God who chose you is holy. For
the Scriptures say, 'You must be holy because I am holy.'"

1 PETER 1:13-16 (NLT)

The elevator doors slid open. As I looked down the long hallway on the hospital floor, for a few seconds I felt rooted to the spot. It had been several months since my last surgery, and I was visiting a friend. This was my first time back since my own visits, and the hallways I'd walked twice a day for weeks looked all too familiar. Fortunately, our visit to the room was short, and while the friends I was with got the latest news from family members, I leaned against the wall, hoping no one would notice that I felt like sliding to the floor.

After that visit, it got easier for me to visit friends in the hospital. I don't mind at all anymore, and it doesn't scare me. I do remember what it's like to be a patient, but I also know that having the courage to visit and smile and encourage—even for only a few minutes—is worth it.

One thing I've learned over the years is that I can't wait to serve others until everything in my life is perfect. I don't know what other people are going through; I don't know their story. And I need to have the courage to reach out, encourage, and serve them, even if I'm going through my own times of pain. That's part of being a follower of Jesus. I listen to Him and obey what He says. Yes, I get support for my own struggles, but when He puts someone on my heart to reach out to, I need to be brave and obey, even if it feels uncomfortable. We never know what our obedience in reaching out and connecting will mean to someone else.

Hopefully you find yourself in a different place than you were eight weeks ago when you started this book. Maybe your circumstances haven't changed, but your heart is learning to hold onto hope. You are full of the hope brought through Jesus.

The word for "holy" in today's verse means "set apart." It doesn't matter what situation you find yourself in, you are set apart for a purpose. Your presence matters. Your love matters. Your perseverance matters. You bring something to the table no one else can because of God's Holy Spirit in you. And you may be able to minister to someone else even deeper because of what you've been through.

So step out into this world knowing that you are not alone. Bravely choose to practice perseverance every day, trusting in God to give you strength. Keep choosing to persevere, and firmly grab hold of the sacred tenacity He has placed within you through His Holy Spirit. He has good plans for you. You are dearly loved by God and called to great things.

PRACTICE PERSEVERANCE: What is one way you can reach out and encourage someone who is struggling today? How do you think your own struggles will help you in ministering to them? Be strong and courageous. Your love matters.

Epilogue

"The Lord bless you

and keep you;

the Lord make His face shine on you

and be gracious to you;

the Lord turn His face toward you

and give you peace."

NUMBERS 6:23–26 (NIV)

Thank You

Sam O'Neal (editor)—Thank you for saying yes to this book and helping make it the best it could be.

Krista Joy Johnson (cover art and interior layout designer)—Thank you for working with excellence and for the incredible cover design.

Steve and Cynthia (my dad and mom)—Thank you for teaching me to be faithful in the little things.

Pop-pop and Grandmama (my dad's parents)—Thank you for your chats on the phone, your stories, and your unconditional support.

Mark, Kathy, Brad, and Julie—Thank you for all of your encouragement, loving correction, prayers, and for helping me finally believe who God says I am.

The Wednesday prayer group ladies, past and present—Thank you for teaching me how to pray.

Contact

Email: sacredtenacitybook@gmail.com
Facebook (Author Page) – www.facebook.com/sacredtenacitybook
Instagram: @heatherdillard35

Made in the USA
Columbia, SC
23 September 2019